Using
Publisher 2019

2019 Edition

Kevin Wilson

Elluminet Press
www.elluminetpress.com

Using Publisher 2019

Publisher: Elluminet Press
Director: Kevin Wilson
Lead Editor: Steven Ashmore
Technical Reviewer: Mike Taylor, Robert Ashcroft
Copy Editors: Joanne Taylor, James Marsh
Proof Reader: Mike Taylor
Indexer: James Marsh
Cover Designer: Kevin Wilson

eBook versions and licenses are also available for most titles. Any source code or other supplementary materials referenced by the author in this text is available to readers at

`www.elluminetpress.com/resources`

For detailed information about how to locate your book's source code, go to

`www.elluminetpress.com/resources`

Table of Contents

About the Author

With over 15 years' experience in the computer industry, Kevin Wilson has made a career out of technology and showing others how to use it. After earning a master's degree in computer science, software engineering, and multimedia systems, Kevin has held various positions in the IT industry including graphic & web design, programming, building & managing corporate networks, and IT support.

He currently serves as Elluminet Press Ltd's senior writer and director, he periodically teaches computer science at college in South Africa and serves as an IT trainer in England. His books have become a valuable resource among the students in England, South Africa and our partners in the United States.

Kevin's motto is clear: "If you can't explain something simply, then you haven't understood it well enough." To that end, he has created the Essential Computing series, in which he breaks down complex technological subjects into smaller, easy-to-follow steps that students and ordinary computer users can put into practice.

Acknowledgements

Thanks to all the staff at Luminescent Media & Elluminet Press for their passion, dedication and hard work in the preparation and production of this book.

To all my friends and family for their continued support and encouragement in all my writing projects.

To all my colleagues, students and testers who took the time to test procedures and offer feedback on the book

Finally thanks to you the reader for choosing this book. I hope it helps you to use your computer with greater understanding.

Microsoft Publisher

Microsoft Publisher is a desktop publishing application developed by Microsoft. Publisher is considered an entry level desktop publishing application and is aimed at home users, schools, and small businesses with in house printing. Publisher is not used for commercial printing purposes.

Publisher differs from Microsoft Word in that the emphasis is placed on page layout and design rather than text composition and proofing.

With Publisher, you can easily create many different types of publication.

Publisher offers various features and tools to create and edit publications such as flyers, banners, greeting cards, posters, and letter heads. These tools are all grouped into tabs in a menu system along the top of the screen called a ribbon.

Publisher uses a WYSIWYG (what-you-see-is-what-you-get) interface, meaning everything you create on screen appears the same way when printed.

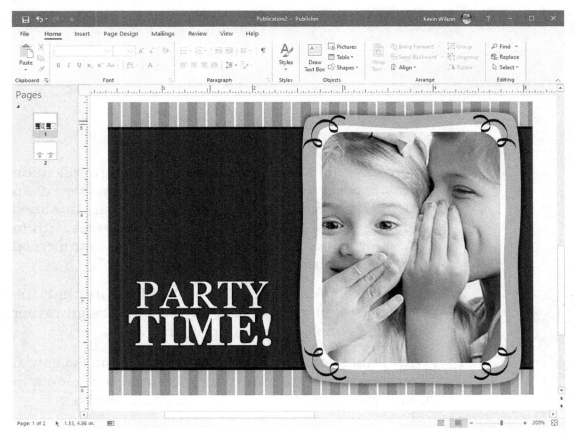

Publisher allows you to freely layout your designs on the page using objects such as text boxes for headings and body text, image placeholders for photographs, and shapes.

Publisher also includes pre-designed templates, and building blocks for creating larger publications called 'page parts'.

Proofing tools such as spell checkers, grammar check allow you to check your work as you type. Potentially misspelled words are underlined in red, grammar errors are marked in green. Auto-correct features correct commonly misspelled words or phrases.

Getting around Publisher

Microsoft Publisher is a desktop publishing application developed by Microsoft. Publisher is considered an entry level desktop publishing application and is aimed at home users, schools, and small businesses with in house printing. Publisher is not used for commercial printing purposes.

Publisher differs from Microsoft Word in that the emphasis is placed on page layout and design rather than text composition and proofing.

With Publisher, you can easily create business cards, flyers, booklets, greeting cards, personalised calendars using your own photographs, graphics, and text.

Getting Started

You can start Publisher 2019 by searching for it using Cortana's search field on your task bar. Type in 'Publisher'. Then click 'Publisher' desktop app as highlighted below.

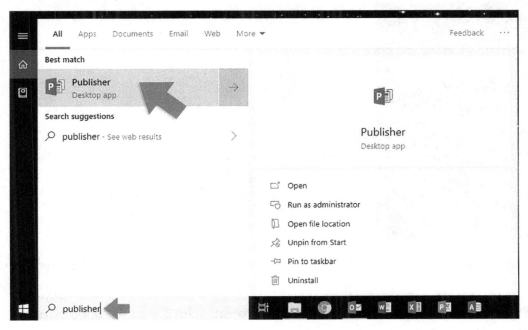

Create a Shortcut

To make things easier, you can pin the Publisher icon to your task bar. I find this feature useful. To do this, right click on the Publisher icon on your taskbar and click 'pin to taskbar'.

This way, Publisher is always on the taskbar whenever you need it.

Chapter 2: Getting around Publisher

Once Publisher has started, select a template from the thumbnails on the right hand side. Click on one to start.

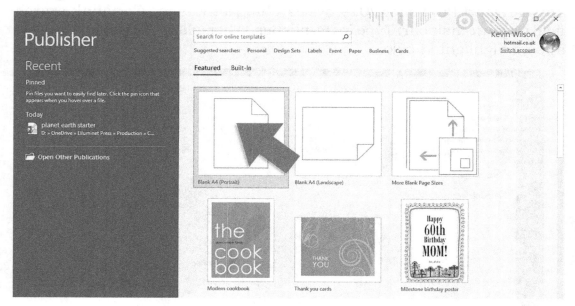

Your most recently saved publications are shown on the left hand green pane.

Lets take a look at Publisher's main screen. Here we can see, illustrated below, the screen is divided into sections.

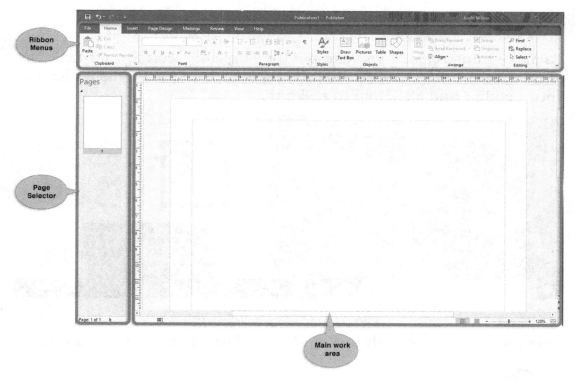

The Ribbon Menus

Your tools are grouped into tabs called ribbons along the top of the screen. Tools are grouped according to their function.

Home Ribbon

All tools to do with text formatting, for example, making text bold, changing fonts, and the most common tools for text alignment, and formatting.

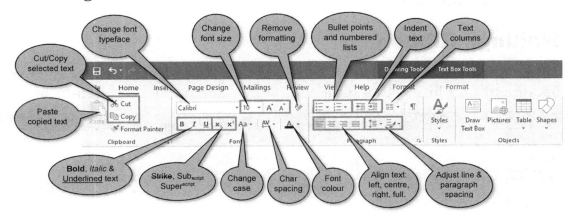

Insert Ribbon

All tools to do with inserting photos, graphics, tables, charts, and borders etc.

You can also insert equations, word art, pre-designed ads, graphic 'page parts', and smart art using the 'illustrations' and 'building blocks' section of the ribbon.

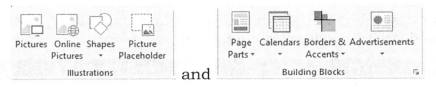 and

You can add text boxes, symbols, and word art using the 'text' section of the ribbon.

Page Design Ribbon

The page design ribbon allows you to change templates, adjust margins, page orientation, size, and set up design guides to help you align the elements on your page.

You can also select pre-designed colour schemes, change the background and set up page masters.

Mailings Ribbon

The mailings ribbon allows you to create mail merges in your publisher document and link it to a data source in a spreadsheet or database.

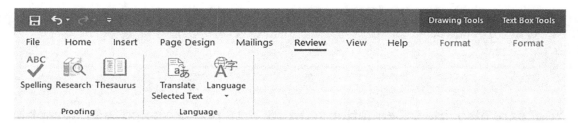

Review Ribbon

With the review ribbon, you can spell check your document, look up words in the thesaurus, translate text into another language, or do some research.

View Ribbon

With the view ribbon you can change your default view, open master pages, add rulers, navigation, and zoom.

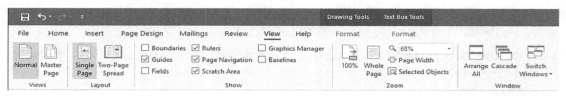

File Backstage

If you click 'File' on the top left of your screen, this will open up what Microsoft call the backstage.

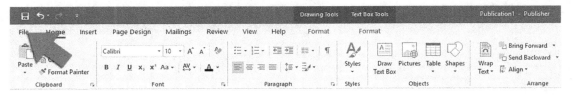

Backstage is where you open or save publications, print, export or share publications, as well as options, Microsoft account and preference settings.

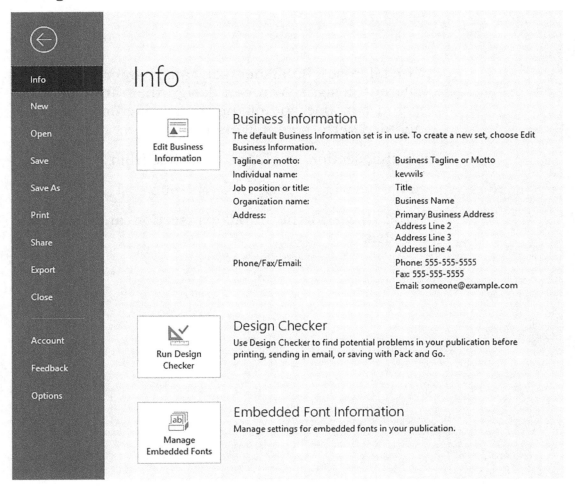

You can also change your Microsoft Account settings, log in and activate your Microsoft Office 2019, change Publisher's preferences and so on.

Building a New Design

With Microsoft Publisher, you can easily create various different designs. You can design them from scratch, or you can use one of the many different templates included with the application.

For this section you'll need the files from

`www.elluminetpress.com/ms-pub`

Scroll down to the publisher section and download the files.

Creating a New Publication

Before you create a new publication you'll need to make a few decisions about certain aspects, such as page layout, paper type, and size.

Some of the first choices you need to make about your publication involve page layout. Creating a publication from a template takes care of most of these choices for you.

Size

Some publications, like flyers, can be small, A5 or A6. Other publications such as posters are a lot bigger, A3 or A1.

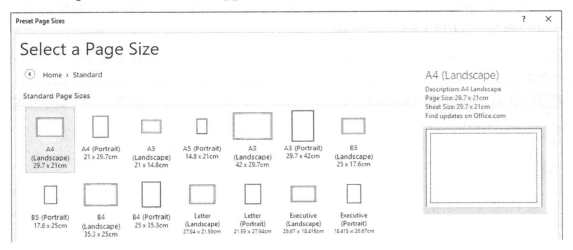

Orientation

Landscape or Portrait. Some flyers are portrait, as are most posters. Greetings cards can be both landscape and portrait orientation.

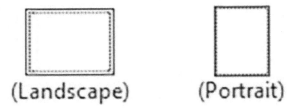

(Landscape)   (Portrait)

Margins

Margins are the areas of blank space around the top, bottom, left and right edges of a printed publication.

Open a New Publication

When you open publisher, you'll be able to select a template to start with or create a blank publication. For this demo, select 'blank A4 (portrait)'.

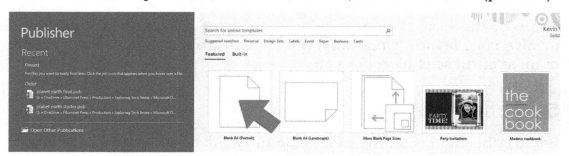

If you already have publisher running, click 'file' on the top left of the main screen, then select 'new'.

Once you've selected a template, you'll land on publisher's main work area.

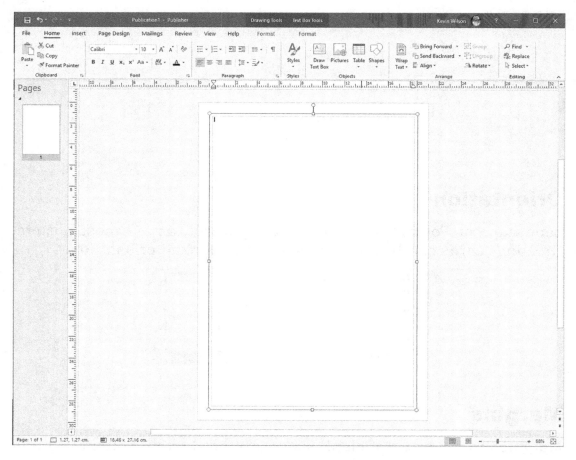

Here, we can start constructing our publication.

The Main Screen

Down the left hand side you'll see your page navigation pane. Here, you can see the number of pages in your publication. Click on the page thumbnail in the navigation pane to jump to that page.

On the bottom left of the screen you'll see three sets of values. The first shows you the page number you're on - click to open and close page navigation pane. The second set shows you the position of the top left corner of an object on your page. So the object selected below is 12.75cm down from the top edge of the page and 4.92cm from the left edge of the page. The last set of numbers shows the size of the selected object.

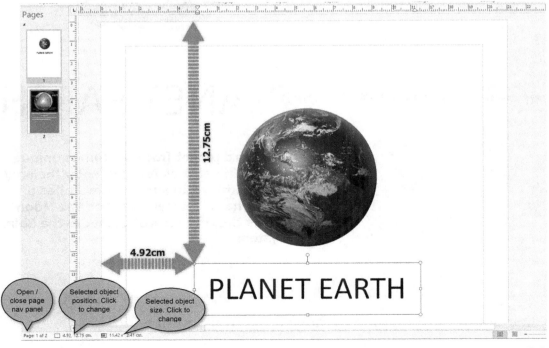

On the bottom right, you'll see your page view and page zoom controls.

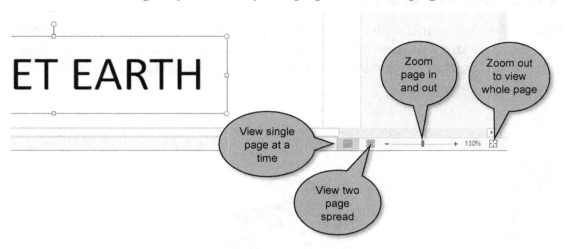

Creating Guides

You can create guide lines to help you align the elements on your design. To do this, click either the horizontal or vertical ruler. Then drag your mouse pointer to the position on your page.

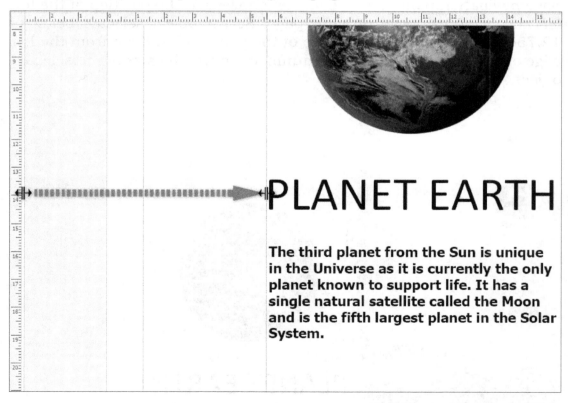

Click and drag the guide to move it again if you need to.

Basic Elements

Publisher documents are constructed using some basic elements. First is the text box.

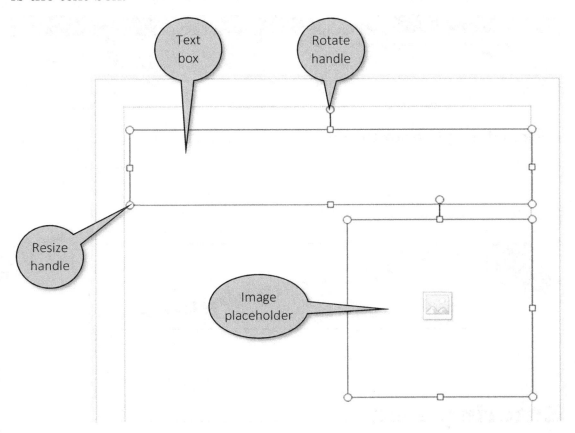

You can add text boxes to your design to contain the text and place it independently.

You can do the same with image place holders. These are used to place images within your design.

These place holders are also called frames. When you click on a frame or place holder, small circles appear around the edge. These are called handles. You can click and drag on the handles to resize your text box or image place holder.

You can also add shapes, charts and tables to your designs.

Lets take a look at the file:

```
planet earth starter.pub
```

Adding a Text Box

To add some text to your design, first you need to add a text box. To add a text box, go to the home ribbon and select 'draw text box'.

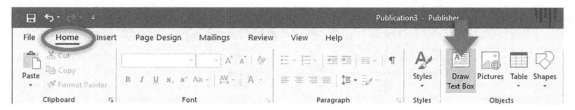

Click and drag to draw the text box on your page

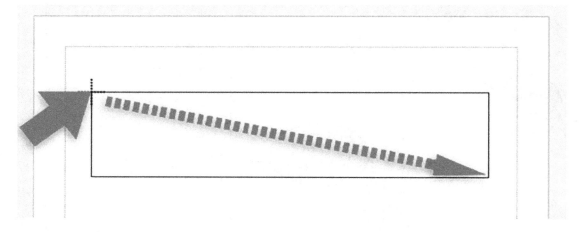

Entering Text

Once you have inserted a text box, you can type in some text.

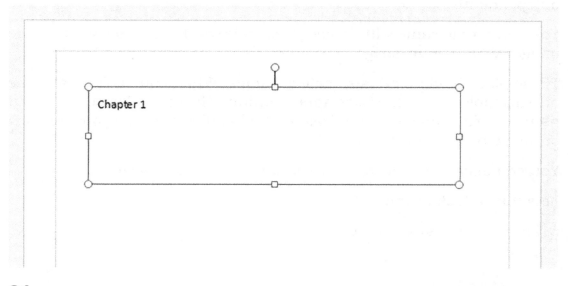

Formatting Text

Within your text box you can format your text. You can do this using the basic formatting tools on the home ribbon.

Changing Font

Highlight the text you want to change.

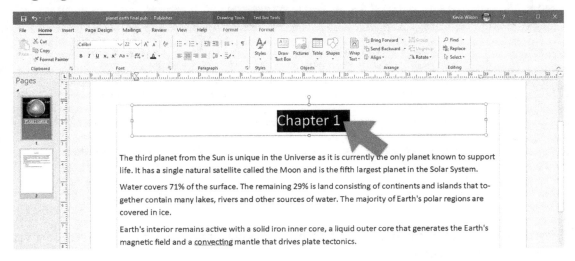

From the home ribbon click on the font name.

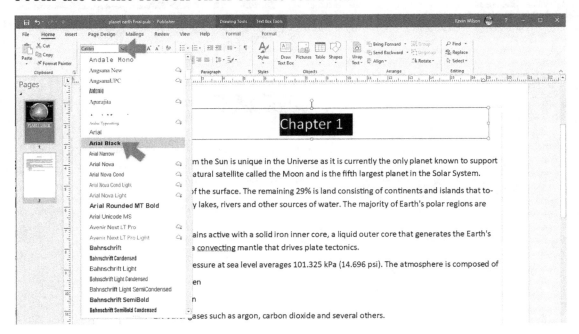

From the drop down box, select the font you want.

Font Size

Highlight the text you want to change.

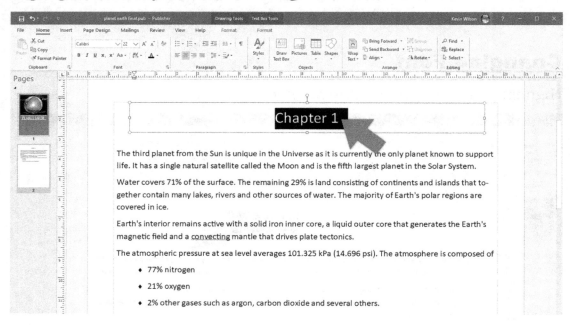

From the home ribbon, select the font size, then from the drop down select the size you want.

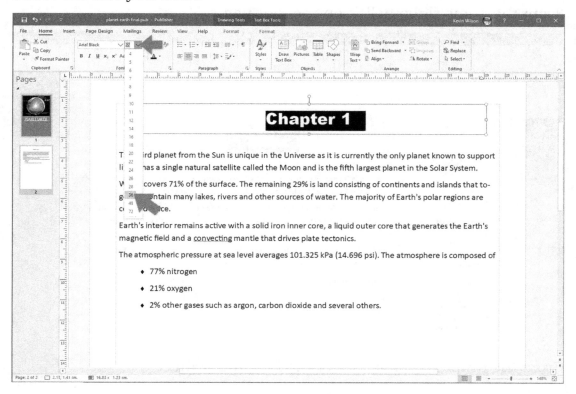

Bold, italic, underlined

Highlight the text you want to change.

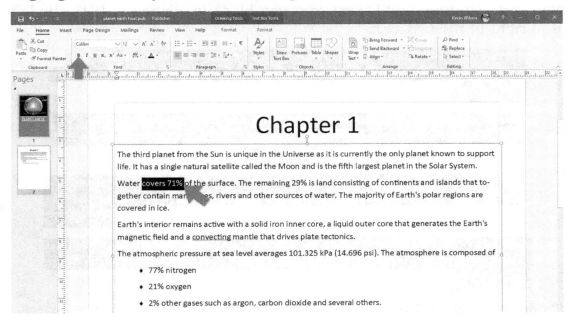

From the home ribbon, click the bold icon on the top left. Do the same for italic and underlined text.

Text Colour

Highlight the text you want to change.

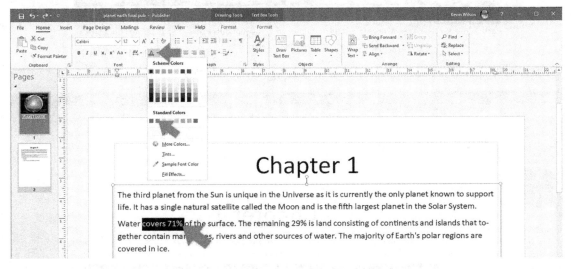

From the home ribbon, select the font colour icon. Select a colour from the drop down box.

Text Alignment

Within your text box you can align text to the left, middle, or the right. You can also fully justify text so a text block is aligned to both the left and right of the text box.

Water covers 71% of the surface. The remaining 29% is land consisting of continents and islands that together contain many lakes, rivers and other sources of water. The majority of Earth's polar regions are covered in ice.

Water covers 71% of the surface. The remaining 29% is land consisting of continents and islands that together contain many lakes, rivers and other sources of water. The majority of Earth's polar regions are covered in ice.

Water covers 71% of the surface. The remaining 29% is land consisting of continents and islands that together contain many lakes, rivers and other sources of water. The majority of Earth's polar regions are covered in ice.

Water covers 71% of the surface. The remaining 29% is land consisting of continents and islands that together contain many lakes, rivers and other sources of water. The majority of Earth's polar regions are covered in ice.

To do this, select the text you want to align.

Chapter 1

The third planet from the Sun is unique in the Universe as it is currently the only planet known to support life. It has a single natural satellite called the Moon and is the fifth largest planet in the Solar System.

Water covers 71% of the surface. The remaining 29% is land consisting of continents and islands that together contain many lakes, rivers and other sources of water. The majority of Earth's polar regions are covered in ice.

Earth's interior remains active with a solid iron inner core, a liquid outer core that generates the Earth's magnetic field and a convecting mantle that drives plate tectonics.

From the home ribbon, select a paragraph alignment icon.

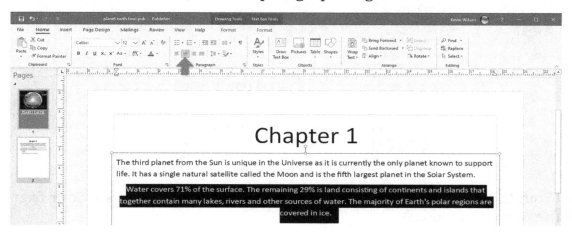

Change Case

You can quickly change the case of your text. You can change it to UPPERCASE, lowercase or Sentence case. To do this, select your text.

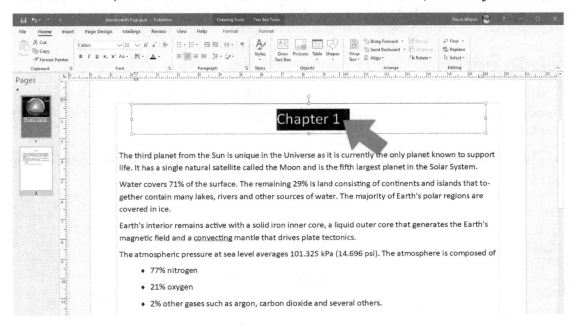

From the home ribbon, select the case change icon.

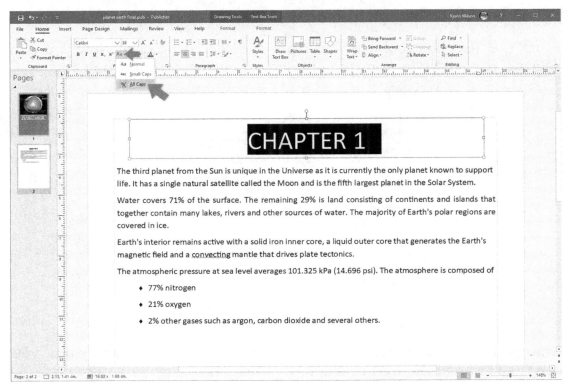

Typography Features

Publisher includes various typography features to help you format your text. It's important to note that these effects only work with certain fonts, such as Calibri, Cambria, Gabriola, Garamond, and Zapfino.

Drop Cap

A drop cap enlarges the first letter of the selected text and is often used at the start of a chapter or block of text. To do this, click on the paragraph you want to drop cap.

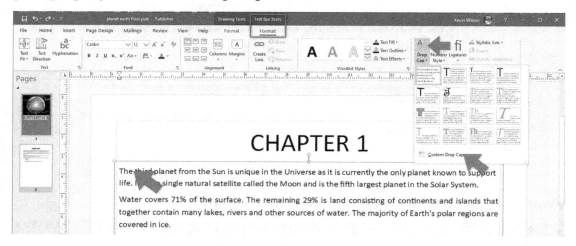

From the 'text box tools' format ribbon, select 'drop cap'. Now you can select a pre-set style from the options, or click 'custom drop cap'.

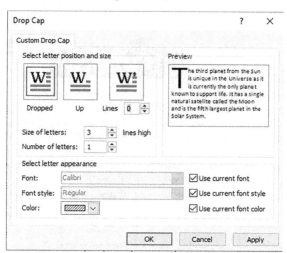

Change the size of letters to fit your drop cap into the paragraph, you can also change the font and colour. Click 'apply' when you're done.

Stylistic Sets

These sets allow you choose between various styles for your fonts, usually in the form of exaggerated serifs or flourishes. Highlight the letter, then from the 'text box tools' format ribbon select 'stylistic sets'

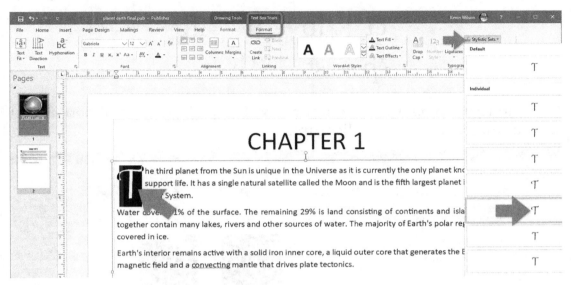

Select an option from the drop down box.

You can also use stylistic sets on words. Useful for creating fancy titles and headings.

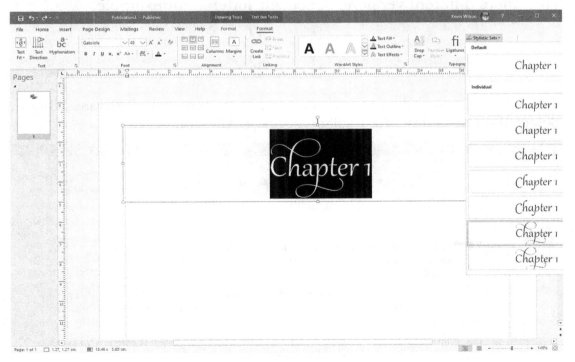

Ligatures

Ligatures connect certain combinations of letters to make them easier to read. There are many different ligatures: ct, ff, fi, ffi, st, sp, Th being the most common.

ct fb ff ffb

sp st Th

You can turn on ligatures from the 'text box tools' format ribbon. Select the character, then select 'ligatures'.

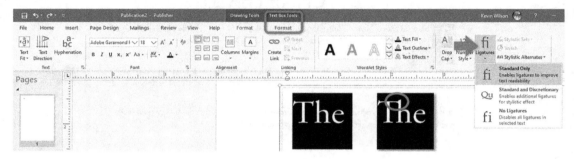

Stylistic Alternates

This offers different versions of specific letters. For example,

a a
g g

You'll find these alternatives on your 'text box tools' format ribbon. Select the character, then select 'stylistic Alternates'.

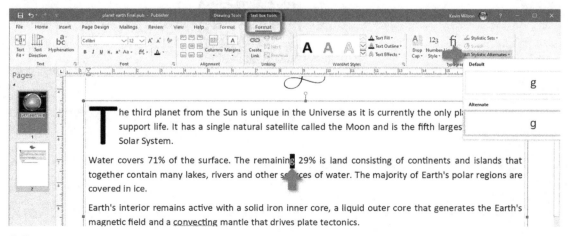

Text Effects

You can add drop shadows, reflections and bevels to your text, as well as change the style, add an outline and fill colour.

Shadows

To add a shadow, select the text you want to use, then from the 'text box tools' format ribbon, select 'text effects'.

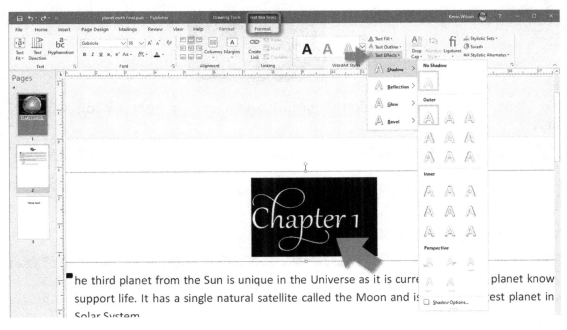

Select an effect from the list. You can also add a reflection, glow, or bevel effect from here.

Text Outline

To add a outline, select the text you want to use, then from the 'text box tools' format ribbon, select 'text outline'.

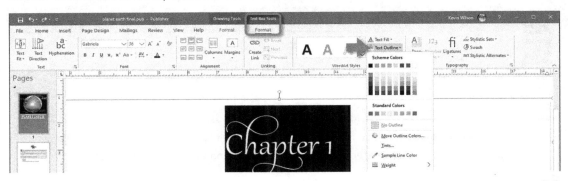

WordArt Styles

To use a wordart style, select the text you want to use, then from the 'text box tools' format ribbon, select a style from the wordart.

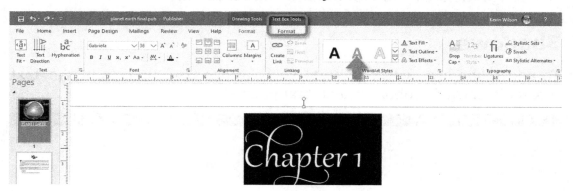

To view more styles, click the small down arrow next to the wordart styles.

You'll see the full list of options.

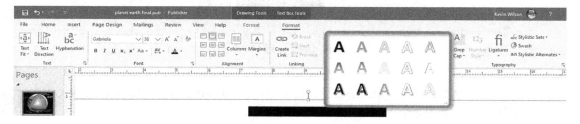

Select a style. You can select from a number of pre-defined styles.

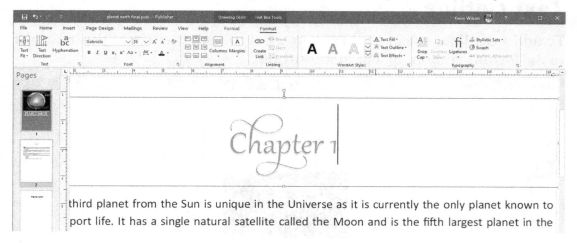

third planet from the Sun is unique in the Universe as it is currently the only planet known to port life. It has a single natural satellite called the Moon and is the fifth largest planet in the

Formatting Text Boxes

You can add drop shadows, reflections and bevels to your text boxes, as well as change the style, add an outline and fill colour.

Background Colour

Select text box, then under 'drawing tools' select the 'format' ribbon. Select 'shape fill'.

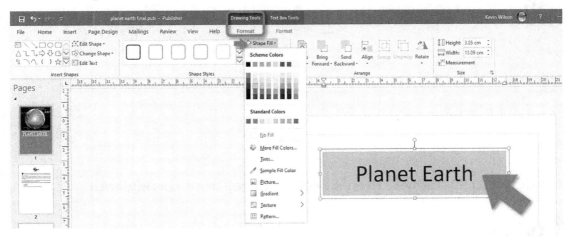

From the drop down menu, select a colour.

Borders

Select text box, then under 'drawing tools' select the 'format' ribbon. Select 'shape outline'.

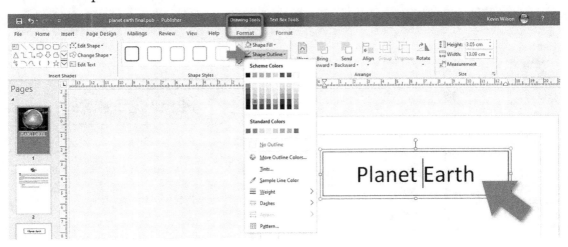

From the drop down menu, select a colour.

35

Shadows

Select text box, then under 'drawing tools' select the 'format' ribbon. Select 'shape effects'.

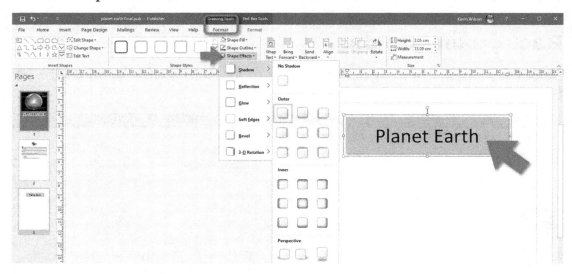

Go down to 'shadows', then select an effect from the slideout.

Styles

There are various pre-defined styles you can use to decorate your text boxes. To apply them, select text box, then under 'drawing tools' select the 'format' ribbon. Click the small arrow next to shape styles to open the panel.

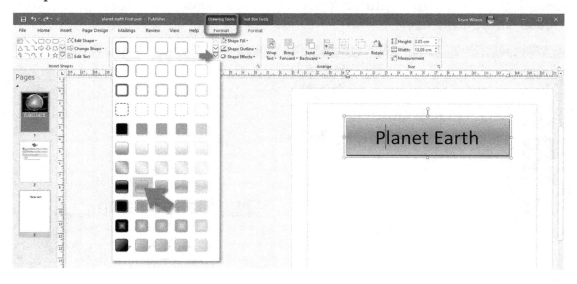

Select a style.

Manipulating Text Boxes

You can move, resize, and rotate text boxes, as well as change the text direction, margins and alignment.

Move Text Box

To move a text box, click on the text box's border. Drag the box to its new location.

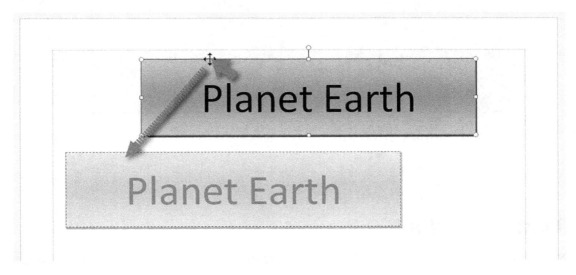

Resize Text Box

To resize a text box, click and drag one of the resize handles until the box is the desired size.

Rotate Text Box

To rotate a text box, click and drag the rotate handle on the top middle of the text box. Drag your mouse left or right to adjust rotation.

Text Direction

You can change the direction of the text in a text box. To rotate your text, select the text box, then from the 'text box tools' format ribbon, click 'text direction'.

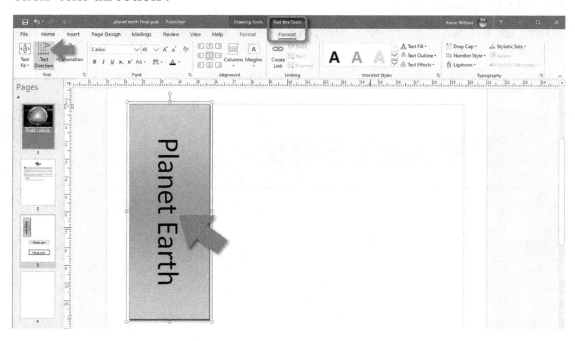

Text Autofit

You can automatically size and fit text inside your text boxes. To do this, select the text box you want to modify, then from the 'format' ribbon under 'text box tools', select 'text fit'.

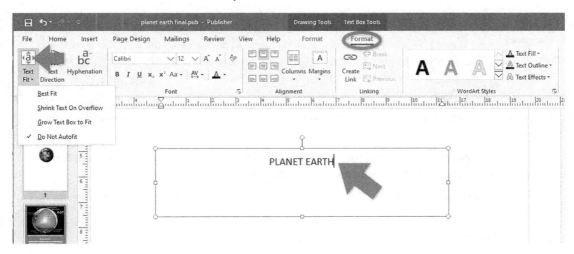

From the drop down menu, select an option.

Best fit makes the text larger or smaller to fit the text box.

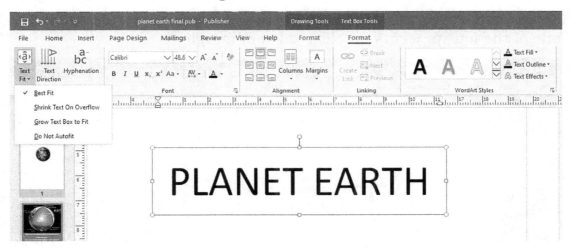

Shrink text on overflow automatically shrinks the text as you type to fill the size of the text box.

Grow text box to fit automatically increases the size of the text box according to the size of the text.

Do not autofit makes no automatic changes to the text or text box size. This is the default option.

Text Box Margins

You can adjust the margins within a text box. The margin is the gap between the text and the edge of the text box. To adjust the margin, click the text box.

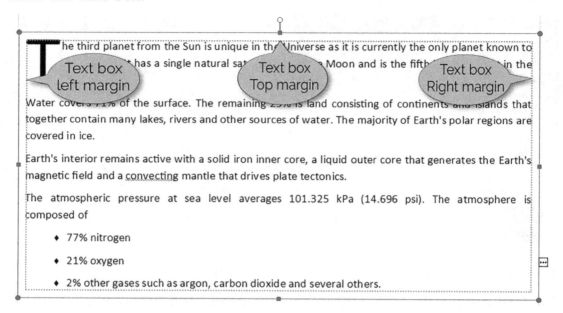

From the 'text box tools' format ribbon, select 'margins'. You can select one of the four presents, or click 'custom margins'.

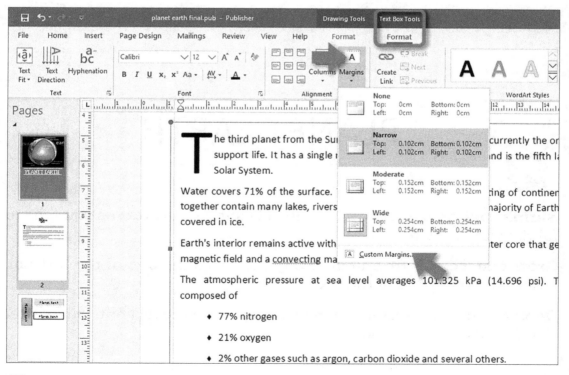

From here, you can individually adjust each of the four margins.

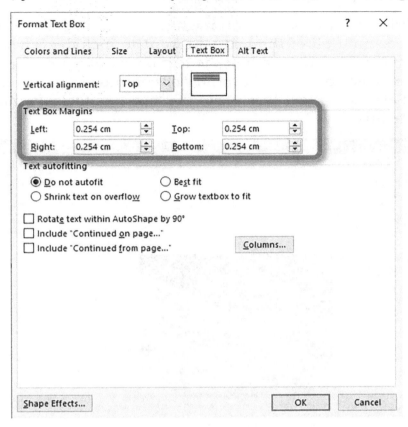

Alignment

You can align your text inside your text box. You can align to the left, middle, right, top, middle or bottom. To do this, click your text box, then from the 'text box tools' format ribbon, select the alignment icon from the alignment section on the ribbon.

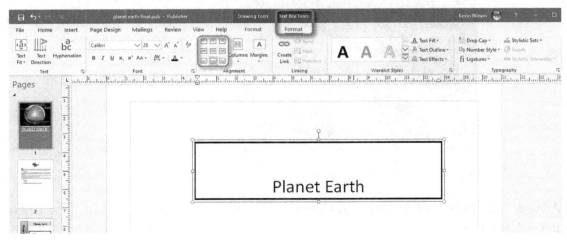

Connecting Text Boxes

As you work with text boxes, you might find that a text box isn't large enough to contain all of the text you want to include. When you run out of room for text, you can link the text boxes. Once two or more text boxes are connected, text will overflow or continue from one text box to the next. Select your text box. From the 'text box tools' format ribbon, click 'create link'.

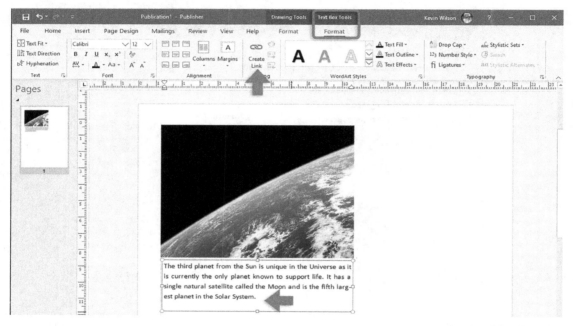

Your mouse pointer will turn into a 'link icon'. Click the position on your page where you want to link to.

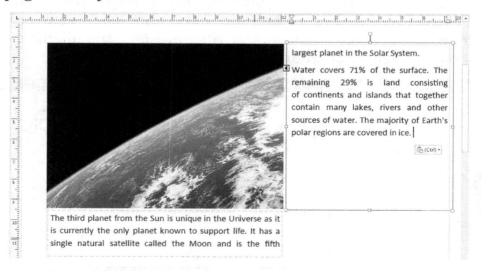

A new text box will appear. As you type your text, the text will flow onto the other text box.

Tables

We have added some more text about world population to our document. Now we want to add a table to illustrate our text.

To insert a table, go to your insert ribbon and select table.

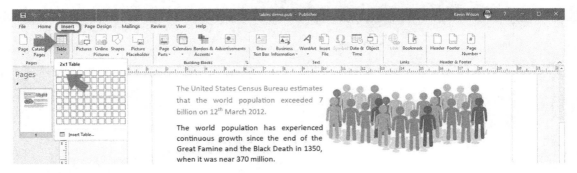

In the grid that appears highlight the number of rows and columns you want. For this table, 1 row and 2 columns.

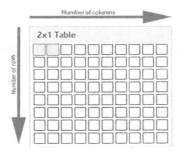

This will add a table with 1 row & 2 columns to your document.

Drag the table into position and enter your data. To move between cells on the table press the tab key. When you get to the end of the row, pressing tab will insert a new row.

Total annual births were highest in the late 1980s at about 139 million and is now expected to remain essentially constant at their 2011 level of 135 million, while deaths number 56 million per year, and are expected to increase to 80 million per year by 2040.

Country	Population
China	1,372,000,000
India	1,276,900,000
USA	321,793,000
Indonesia	252,164,800
Brazil	204,878,000

Resize Table

To resize a table, click and drag one of the corners of the grey border.

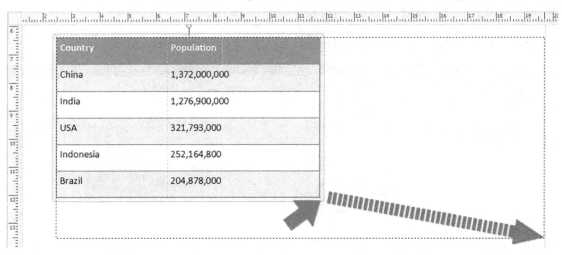

Move Table

To move your table, click anywhere on the table, then click and drag the grey border.

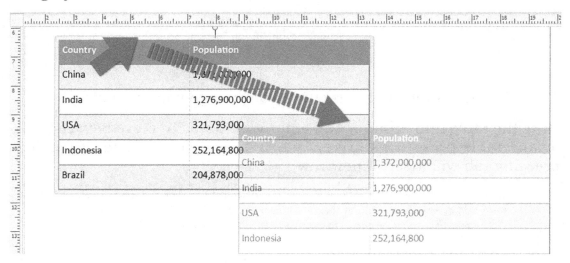

Formatting Tables

When you click on a table in your document, two new ribbons appear under 'table tools': design and layout.

The design ribbon allows you to select pre-set designs for your table, such as column and row shading, borders, and colour.

In the centre of your design ribbon, you'll see a list of designs. Click the small arrow on the bottom right of the 'table styles' panel to open it up.

For this table, I am going to choose one with blue headings and shaded rows.

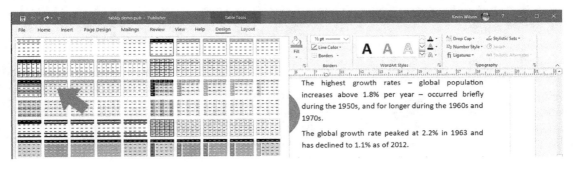

The highest growth rates – global population increases above 1.8% per year – occurred briefly during the 1950s, and for longer during the 1960s and 1970s.

The global growth rate peaked at 2.2% in 1963 and has declined to 1.1% as of 2012.

Add a Column

You can add a column to the right hand side of the table. To do this, click in the end column.

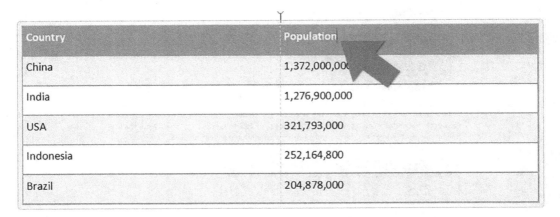

Country	Population
China	1,372,000,000
India	1,276,900,000
USA	321,793,000
Indonesia	252,164,800
Brazil	204,878,000

Select the layout ribbon under 'table tools', and select 'insert right'.

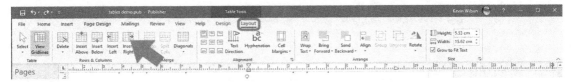

This inserts a column to the right of the one you selected. Resize your table if needed.

Insert a Row

To add a row, click on the row where you want to insert. For example, I want to add a row between USA and Indonesia. So click on Indonesia, as shown below.

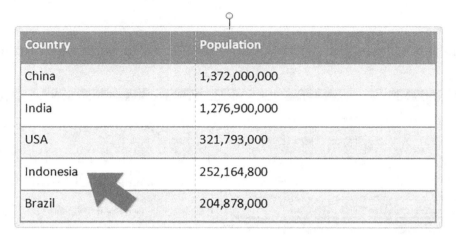

Select the layout ribbon from the table tools section.

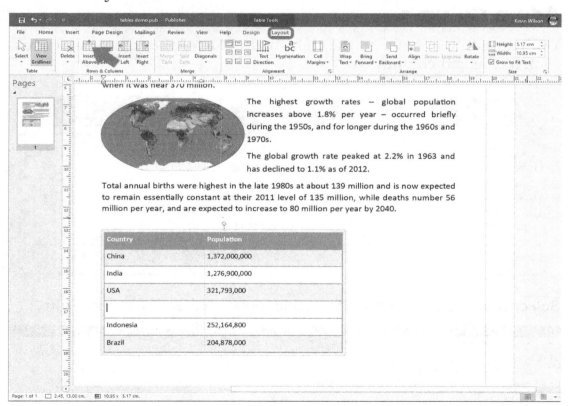

Click 'insert above'. This will insert a row above the one you selected earlier.

Resizing Rows & Columns

You can resize the column or row by clicking and dragging the row or column dividing line to the size you want.

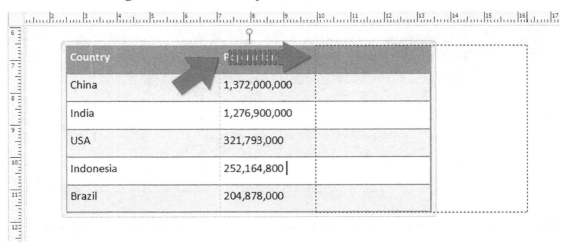

Merge Cells

You can merge cells together. To do this, select the cells you want to merge.

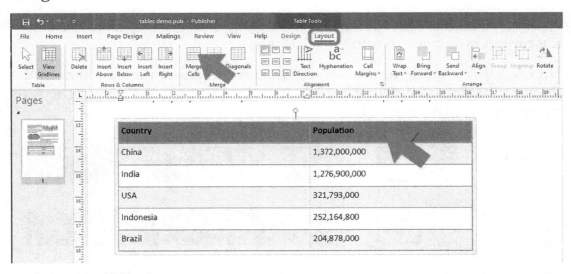

Then select 'merge cells' from the layout ribbon in the table tools section.

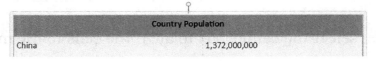

All the selected cells will be merged into a single cell.

Align Cell Text

You can change text alignment in the cells of the table. To do this, select the cells you want to align. Click and drag...

Country	Population	Percentage of World
China	1,372,000,000	18.5
India	1,276,900,000	17.5
USA	321,793,000	4.35
Indonesia	252,164,800	3.35
Brazil	204,878,000	2.77

Select the layout ribbon in the table tools section, as shown below.

From the alignment section, use the nine boxes to select the text alignment you want to apply to the cells.

Here's a quick guide to what the 9 different alignments look like. In the diagram below, note where each box on the left puts the text in the cells in the example on the right.

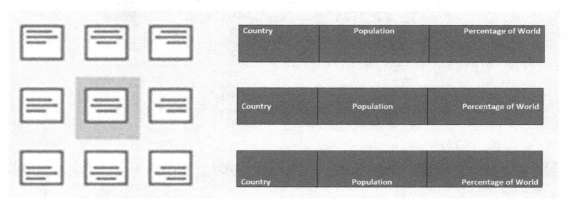

For example, select the center box to align the cells to the middle of the cell.

Cell Border

Select the cells you want to add a border to.

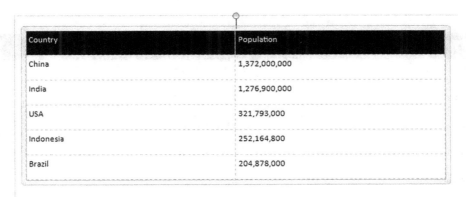

Click the 'table tools' design tab. Select a line thickness

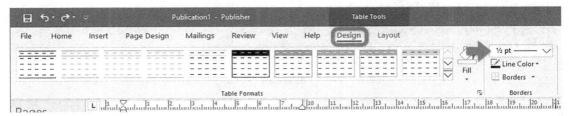

Select a line colour

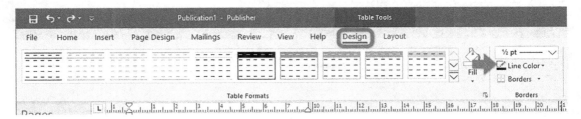

Click 'borders'. From the drop down, select where on your selection you want the borders to appear.

Cell Colour

Select the cell or cells you want to change colour

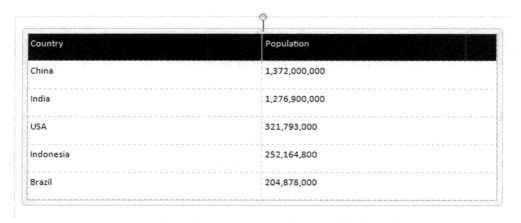

Click 'table tools' design tab.

Click the fill. Select a colour from the pallet.

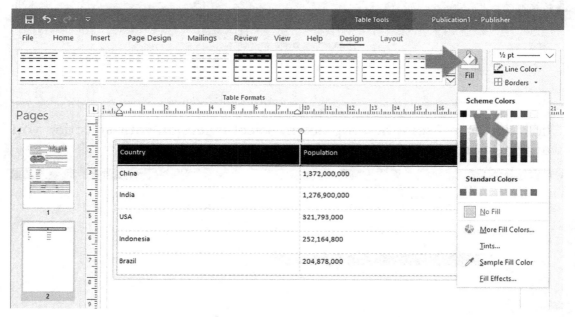

Text Direction

Also you can arrange the text vertically, this usually works for headings.

To do this, select the heading rows in your table.

Country	Population	Percentage of World
China	1,372,000,000	18.5
India	1,276,900,000	17.5
USA	321,793,000	4.35
Indonesia	252,164,800	3.35
Brazil	204,878,000	2.77

From the layout ribbon click 'text direction'.

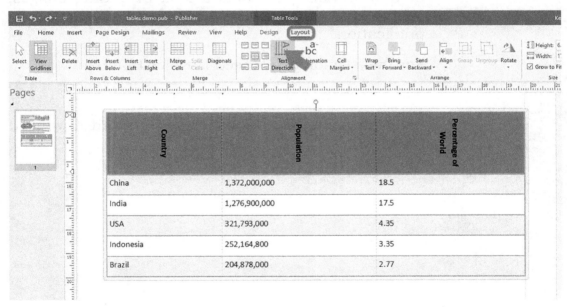

Adding Graphics

In this section, we'll take a look at adding images, shapes and other tools to add some colour to our publication.

For this section you'll need the files from

www.elluminetpress.com/ms-pub

Scroll down to the publisher section and download the files.

Adding Images

Adding images to your document is easy.

There are two ways.

- Your own photos and pictures stored on your computer or OneDrive.

- Clipart. This is a large library of images that can be used in your documents.

Go to your 'insert' ribbon and click on 'Pictures'

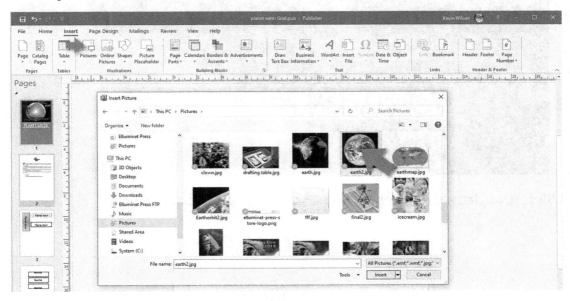

Choose the picture or photo you want from the dialog box that appears. Click insert.

This will insert your photo into your document.

Chapter 4: Adding Graphics

Once imported into Publisher, you may need to resize the image, as sometimes they can come in a bit big. To do this click on the image, you'll see small handles appear on each corner of the image. These are called resize handles. You can use them by clicking and dragging a corner toward the centre of the image to make it smaller as shown below. Hold down the shift key as you resize the image to prevent it from being distorted.

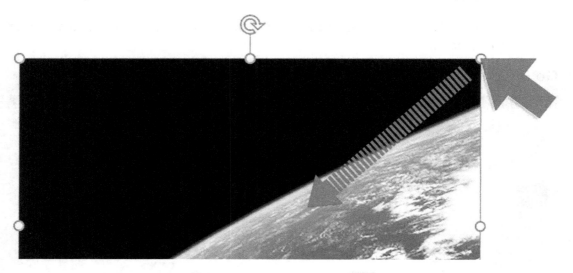

Click and drag the photo into position on your document.

Chapter 1

The third planet from the Sun is unique in the Universe as it is currently the only planet known to support life. It has a single natural satellite called the Moon and is the fifth largest planet in the Solar System.

Water covers 71% of the surface. The remaining 29% is land consisting of continents and islands that together contain many lakes, rivers and other sources of water. The majority of Earth's polar regions are covered in ice.

Earth's interior remains active with a solid iron inner core, a liquid outer core that generates the Earth's magnetic field and a convecting mantle that drives plate tectonics.

Images from Google

You can also search for images on Google. When you download an image, make sure you save them into your pictures folder. Open your web browser and run a google search, then select 'images'.

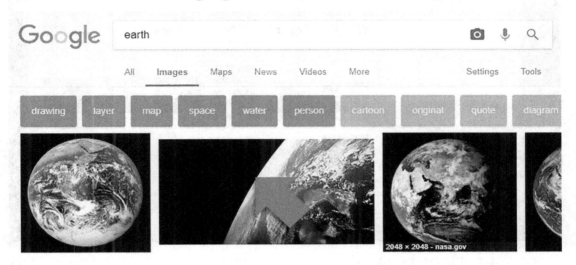

Click on the image thumbnail in the search results to view the full size image. Then right click image, select 'save image as' from the popup menu.

From the dialog box that appears, save the picture into your 'pictures' folder either on your PC or OneDrive folder.

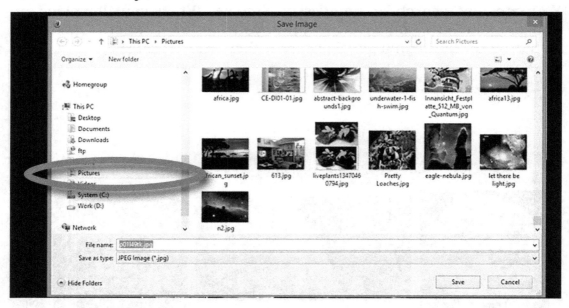

Once your image is saved into your pictures folder, you can import them into your Publisher document using the same procedure at the beginning of the chapter.

Adding Clipart

Carrying on with our document, I want to add a new section called "World Population" and I want some clipart to illustrate this.

To add a clipart image, go to your insert ribbon and click 'online pictures'.

Then, in the dialog box, type in what you are looking for, as shown below. In this example, enter the search term 'population'.

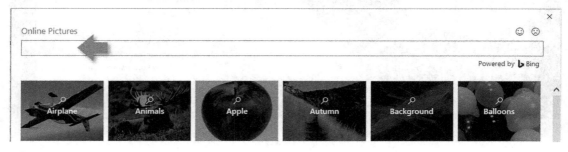

In the search results, click the image you want then click insert.

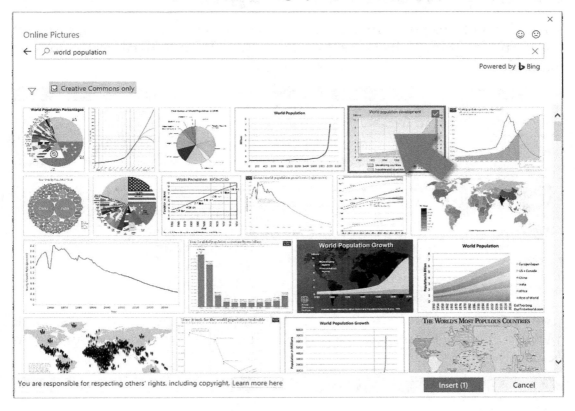

Again, you might need to resize and position the image. Hold down the shift key as you resize the image to prevent it from being distorted.

World Population

The United States Census Bureau estimates that the world population exceeded 7 billion on 12th March 2012.

The world population has experienced continuous growth since the end of the Great Famine and the Black Death in 1350, when it was near 370 million.

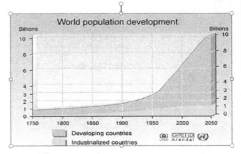

The highest growth rates – global population increases above 1.8% per year – occurred briefly during the 1950s, and for longer during the 1960s and 1970s. The global growth rate peaked at 2.2% in 1963 and has declined to 1.1% as of 2012.

Total annual births were highest in the late 1980s at about 139 million and is now expected to remain essentially constant at their 2011 level of 135 million, while deaths number 56 million per year, and are expected to increase to 80 million per year by 2040.

Adding Effects to Images

To add effects to your images, such as shadows and borders, click on your image, then select the 'picture tools' format b ribbon. In this example, click on the population image.

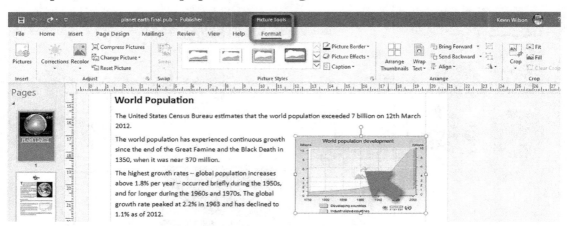

I want to create a nice reflection style to the image. To do this, click 'picture effects', then go down to 'reflection'. Select a variation as shown below.

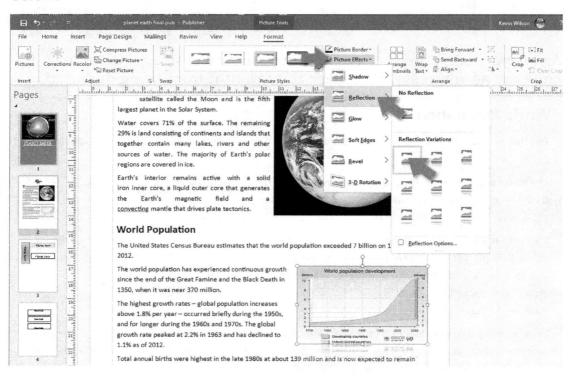

Try different effects, such as 'shadow', 'bevel' or 'glow'. See what effect they have...

Add a Caption

Click the image you want to add the caption to, then from the 'picture tools' format ribbon select 'caption'. From the drop down menu, select a caption style.

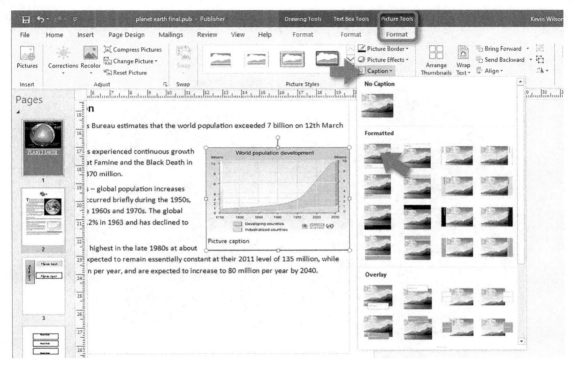

Type in your caption...

World Population

The United States Census Bureau estimates that the world population exceeded 7 billion on 12th March 2012.

The world population has experienced continuous growth since the end of the Great Famine and the Black Death in 1350, when it was near 370 million.

The highest growth rates – global population increases above 1.8% per year – occurred briefly during the 1950s, and for longer during the 1960s and 1970s. The global growth rate peaked at 2.2% in 1963 and has declined to 1.1% as of 2012.

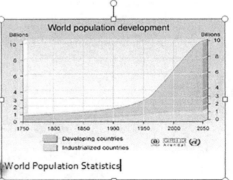

Total annual births were highest in the late 1980s at about 139 million and is now expected to remain essentially constant at their 2011 level of 135 million, while deaths number 56 million per year, and are expected to increase to 80 million per year by 2040.

Cropping Images

If you insert an image into your document, and it has unwanted parts, or you want to concentrate on one particular piece of the picture, you can crop the image

First, insert an image from your pictures library into your document.

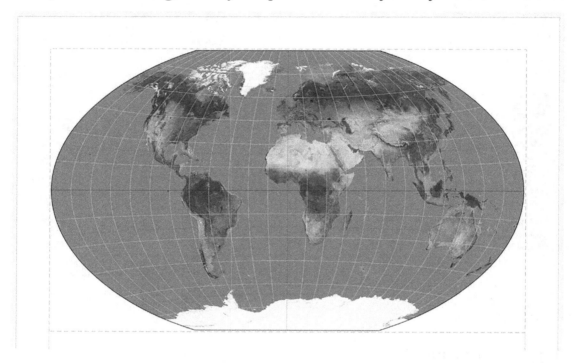

To crop, click on the image, then click the 'picture tools' format ribbon. From the format ribbon, click the crop icon.

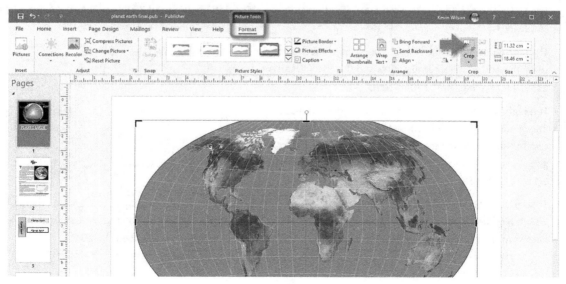

If you look closely at your image, you will see crop handles around the edges, shown circled below.

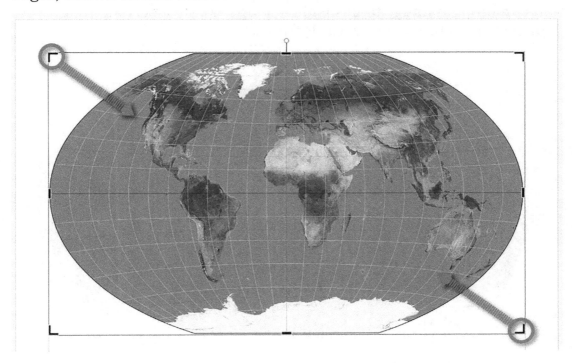

Click and drag these handles around the part of the image you want to keep. Eg, I just want to show Africa in the image.

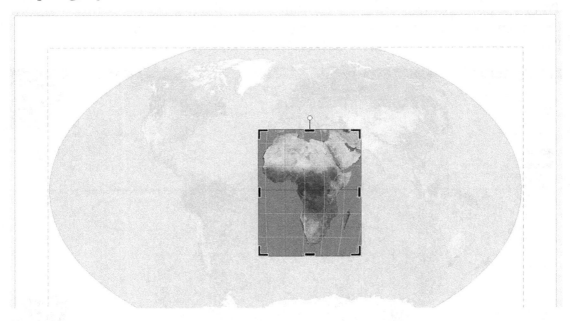

The light grey bits will be removed to leave the bit of the image inside the crop square. Click anywhere on your document to finish.

Crop to Shape

You can crop an image to fit inside a shape. First, insert an image from your pictures library into your document.

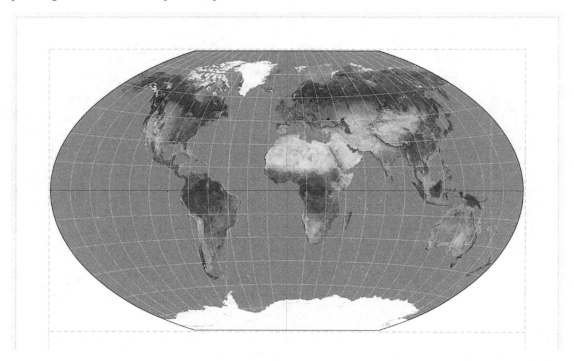

To crop, click on the image, then click the 'picture tools' format ribbon. From the format ribbon, click the down arrow under the crop icon. From the drop down menu, select 'crop to shape'.

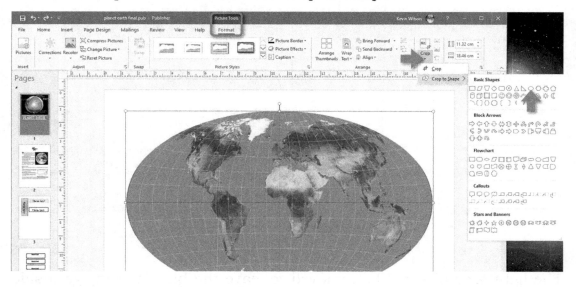

From the slideout, select a shape.

If you look closely at your image, you will see crop handles around the edges, shown circled below. Click and drag these handles around the part of the image you want to keep. Eg, I just want to show Africa in the image.

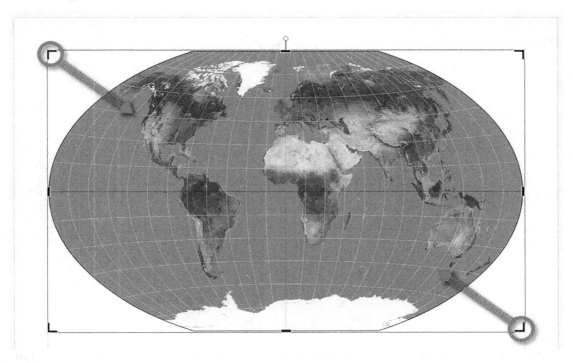

The light grey bits will be removed to leave the bit of the image inside the crop square. Click anywhere on your document to finish.

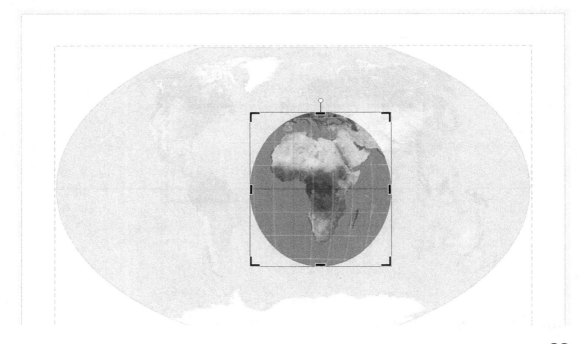

Adjusting Images

You can adjust the brightness and contrast of your images or re-colour them so the image fits into your colour scheme.

To adjust an image, first right click on it. From the popup menu select 'format picture'. From the dialog box, select the 'picture' tab.

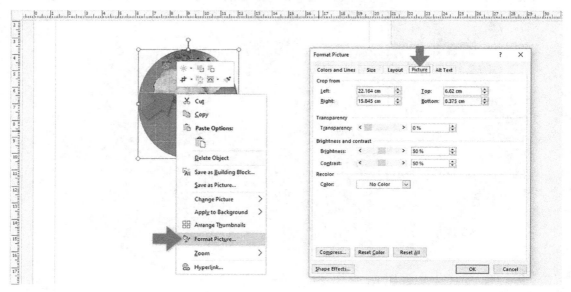

Now, use the transparency slider to change the transparency of the image. Use the brightness & contrast sliders to adjust the brightness and contrast. Use the recolour drop down to change the colour of the image.

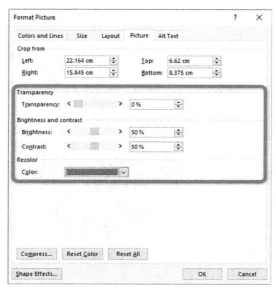

Click 'ok' when you're done.

Wrap Text around Images

When you insert an image, the image will be automatically wrapped with text, meaning the text will arrange itself around the image rather than underneath it or over it.

To change the text wrap, click on the image then from the format ribbon, click 'wrap text'.

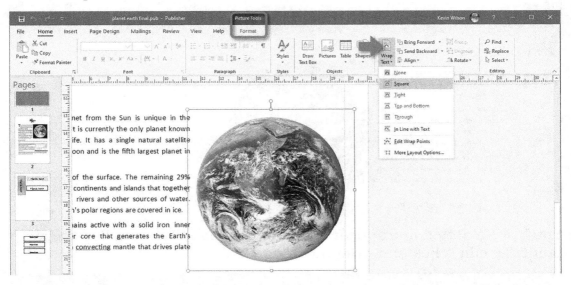

Select 'tight' from the drop down list to align the text squarely around the border of the image.

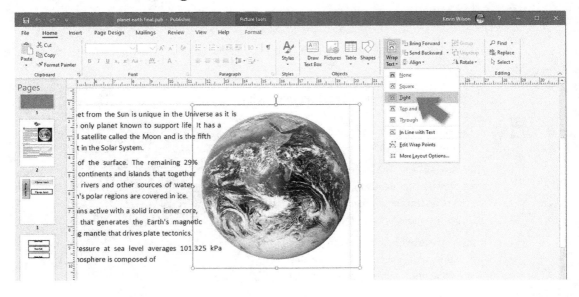

Click and drag the image into position if you need to. As you do this, you'll notice the text will arrange itself around the image.

Wrap Points

You can also customise the points at which the text wraps around the image. To do this, click the image then from the format ribbon, click 'wrap text'. Select 'edit wrap points' from the drop down menu.

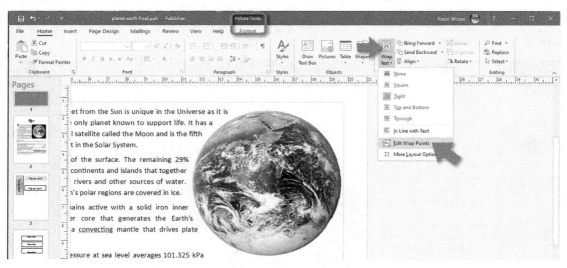

You'll see a dotted line appear around the image. This is called the wrap point. To edit, click and drag the dots.

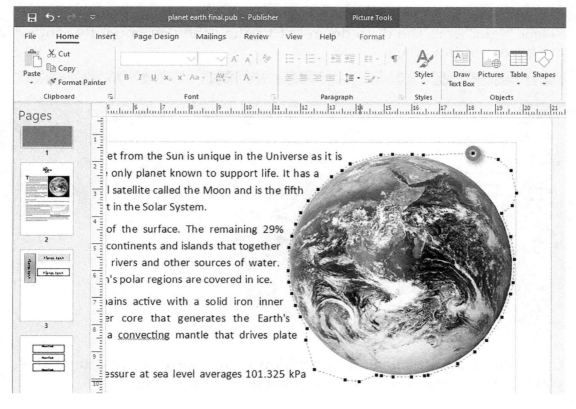

Adding Shapes

You can add various different shapes to your publication. You can add squares, rectangles, circles, lines, speech bubbles, as well as various flow chart symbols.

To insert a shape, select your 'insert' ribbon.

From the dropdown menu, select your shape.

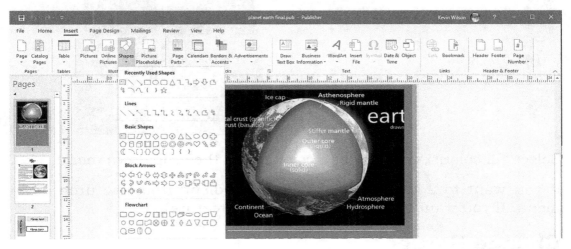

Click and drag your mouse on your document to create the shape.

Modifying Shapes

You can change the colour, outline and add shadows to your shapes.

Change Colour

To change this, click on your shape, then select the 'drawing tools' format ribbon.

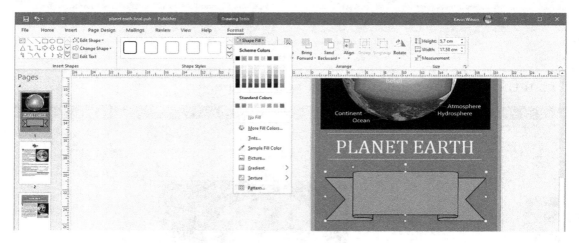

Select 'fill colour', then select a colour from the drop down menu.

If you want to add a gradient, select 'gradient' from the drop down menu. If you want to add a texture, select 'texture'.

Change Border

To change this, click on your shape, then select the 'drawing tools' format ribbon. Select 'shape outline', then select a colour.

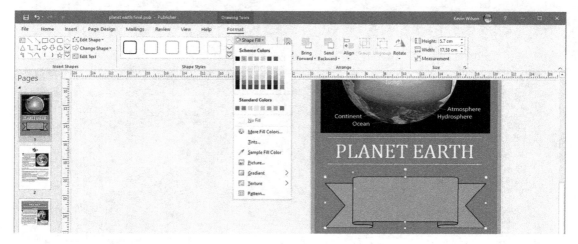

To change the thickness of the border, select 'weight'.

Add a Shadow

To add a shadow, click on your shape, then select the 'drawing tools' format ribbon.

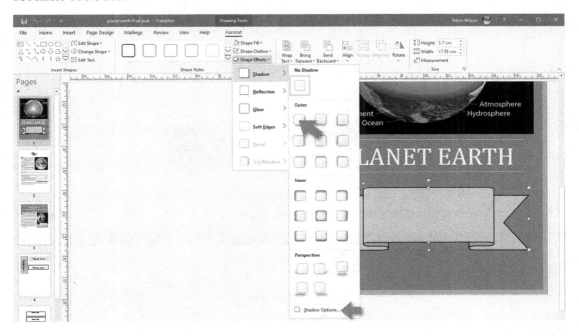

Select 'shape effects', then select an effect from the drop down menu.

To edit the effect, go down to '...options' at the bottom of the slideout menu.

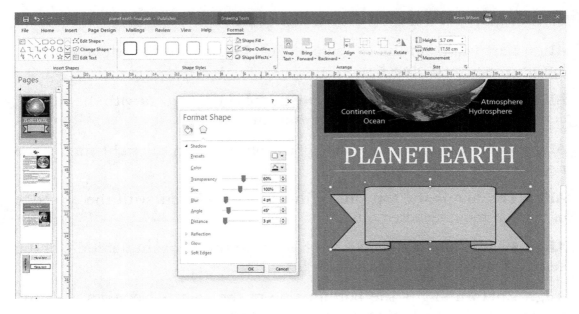

Use the sliders to customise your effect.

Align Objects

You can automatically align objects on your page. To do this, first select all the objects you want to align. Hold down the control key on your keyboard while you click the images you want to align.

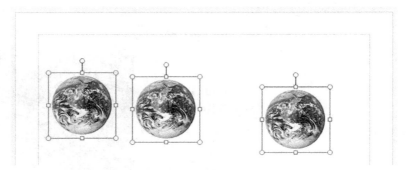

Click the 'picture tools' format ribbon and select 'arrange'. Click 'align'.

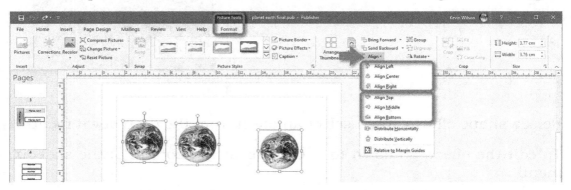

Select an option from the drop down menu.

Align Left will align the left side of the objects with the left edge of the left most selected object.

Align Centre will align the centre of the selected objects with the vertical centre of the selected object that is in the middle.

Align Right aligns the right side of the objects with the right edge of the right most selected object.

Align Top aligns the top side of the selected objects with the top edge of the top most selected object.

Align Middle aligns the selected objects in the horizontal middle of the selected object that is in the middle.

Align Bottom aligns the bottom side of the selected objects with the bottom edge of the bottom most selected object.

Distribute Objects

You can automatically distribute multiple objects evenly across your page. To do this, first select all the objects you want to distribute. Hold down the control key on your keyboard while you click the images you want to distribute.

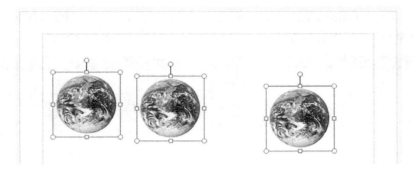

Click the 'picture tools' format ribbon and select 'arrange'. Click 'align'.

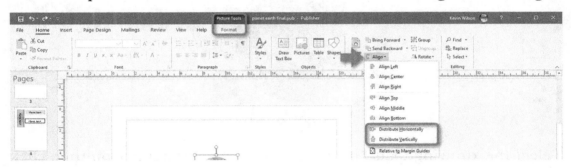

From the drop-down menu, select 'distribute horizontally' or 'distribute vertically'.

Distribute Horizontally will move the selected objects an equal distance apart horizontally across your selection.

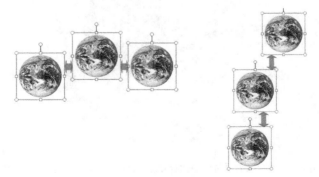

Distribute Vertically will move the selected objects an equal distance apart vertically across your selection.

Group Objects

You can group multiple objects into one object so they stay together if you move them. This is useful if you have created a graphic made up of multiple shapes and objects so you can resize and move without having to adjust each shape.

To do this, first select all the objects you want to group. Hold down the control key on your keyboard while you click the images.

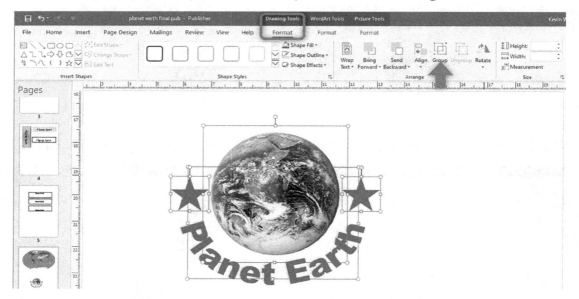

Select the 'drawing tools', or the 'picture tools' format ribbon then click 'group'.

You'll now be able to move the graphic as a single object.

To ungroup, select the object, then from the 'drawing tools' or the 'picture tools' format ribbon, select 'ungroup'.

Arranging Object Layers

Publications are constructed using transparent layers. Every time you add an object, text box, image, or shape you're adding it as a new layer on top. So a design like this:

Will have layers like this:

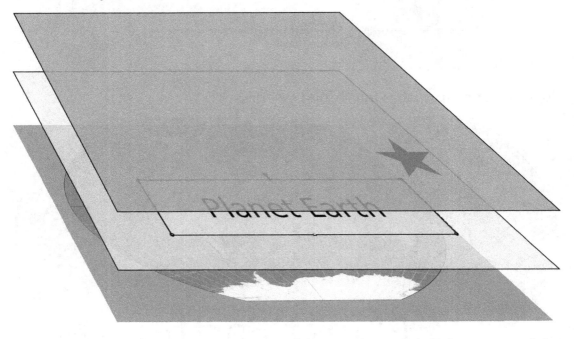

You can see the map is on the bottom layer, the text box is on top of the map, and the star is on top of the text box.

Now, if we wanted the star behind the text box we could change the layer arrangement. Select the star.

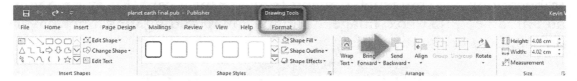

From the 'drawing tools' format ribbon, click 'send backward'.

Now you'll see the layer order change. The star will move behind the text box.

So you'll end up with something like this...

Page Parts

Publisher has some pre-designed building blocks to help you design your page. You can quickly add titles or sidebars to your page, as well as pre-formatted stories and quotes.

To add a page part, select the 'insert' ribbon, then click 'page parts'. Select a template from the drop down menu.

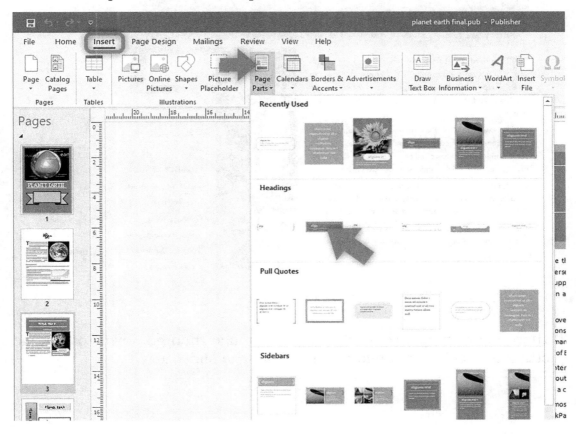

Click and drag the page part into position and resize it if necessary.

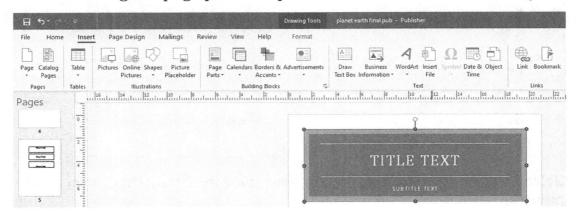

Type in your text in the place holders.

If there is an image, right click on the image then go down to 'change picture' and select 'change picture' from the slideout.

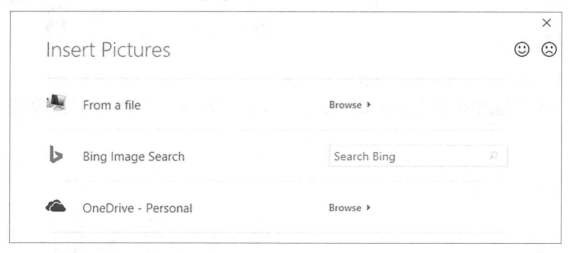

Select where you want to insert your picture from, then select your picture.

If you want to change the colours. Click on the page part, then select the 'drawing tools' format ribbon.

From here you can use the shape fill to change the fill colour, shape outline to change the border colours, and shape effects to add shadows or reflections to the page part.

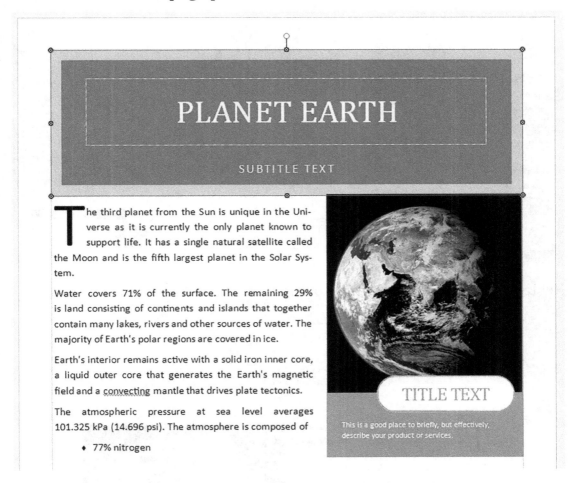

You can also use the shape style presets on this ribbon tab.

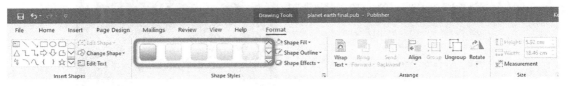

Select one and try it.

Borders & Accents

You can add borders to your page, image or text box. You can also add accents which are small decorations that can be used to emphasise other objects.

To add an accent, select your insert ribbon then click 'borders and accents'.

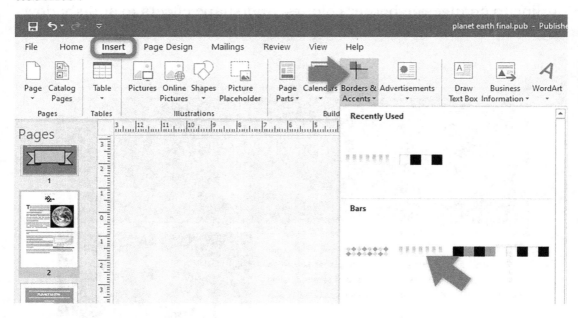

Resize and move the accent into position

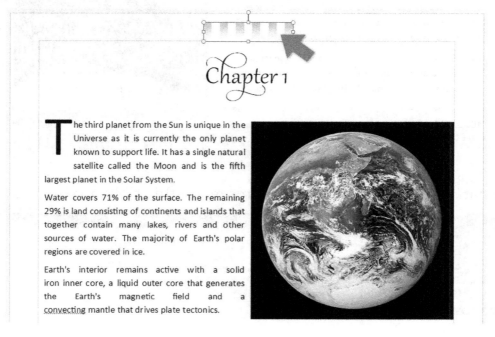

Calendars

To add a calendar, select your insert ribbon then click 'calendars'. Select a template from the drop down menu.

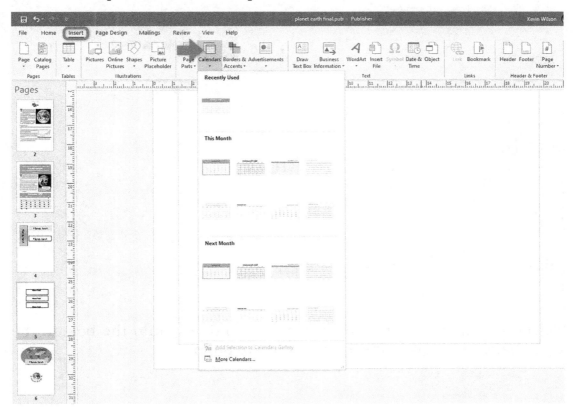

Resize and move your calendar into position.

	December 2019					
MON	TUE	WED	THU	FRI	SAT	SUN
						1
2	3	4	5	6	7	8
9	10	11	12	13	14	15
16	17	18	19	20	21	22
23	24	25	26	27	28	29
30	31					

If you need to add a calendar with a specific month, select 'more calendars' from the calendar drop down menu.

Select a template, then enter the month and year into the box on the right hand side. Click 'insert' when you're done.

Advertisements

You can quickly create ads, attention grabbers, free offers and coupons. To do this, select your insert ribbon then click 'advertisements'. Select a template from the drop down menu. To see all ad templates, click 'more advertisements' at the bottom.

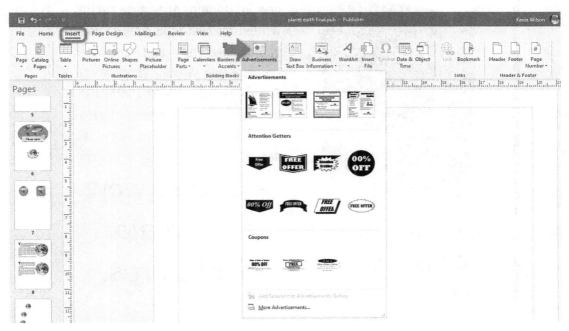

Resize and move the ad into place on your page.

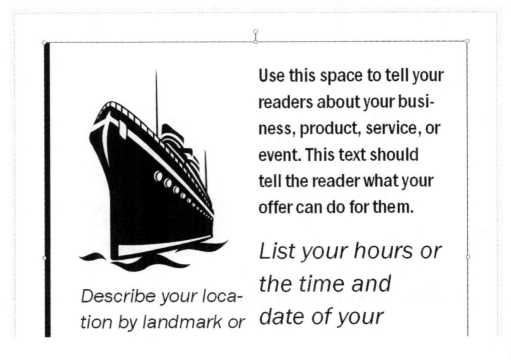

Type your information into the text boxes.

To change any images, right click on the image and click 'change image' then select 'change image' from the slideout.

Select where you want to insert your picture from, then select your picture.

WordArt

WordArt is useful for creating headings and eye catching text. To add WordArt, click the 'insert' ribbon then select 'WordArt'. Select a style from the drop down menu.

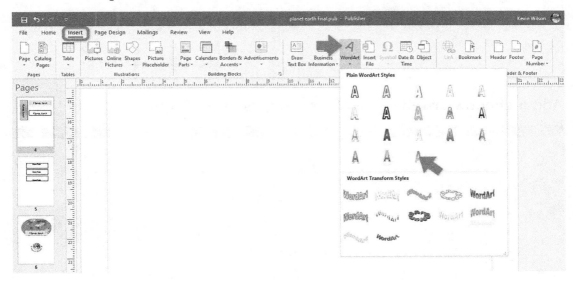

Select your font and size then enter your WordArt text.

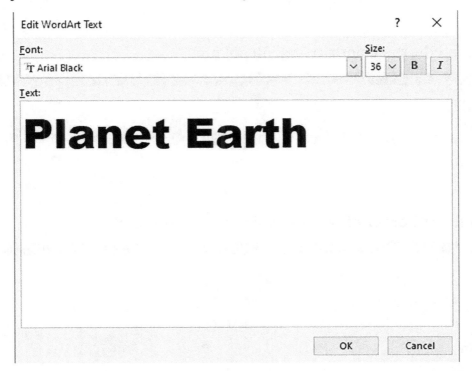

Click 'ok'.

From the WordArt Tools Format ribbon, you can change the style of the text using the presets.

Add a shadow or reflection effect using 'shape effects'.

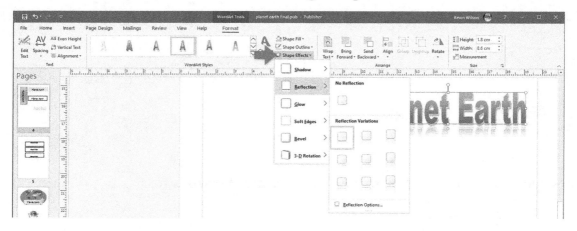

You can edit the colour using 'fill colour'.

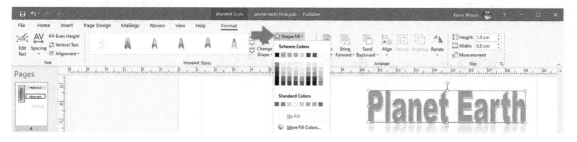

Change the border of the text using 'shape outline'.

You can also change the shape of the text. To do this, click 'change shape'. Select a shape from the drop down menu.

To adjust the shape, click and drag the small yellow handle on the WordArt.

Use the resize handles to resize your WordArt, use the rotate handle to rotate your WordArt.

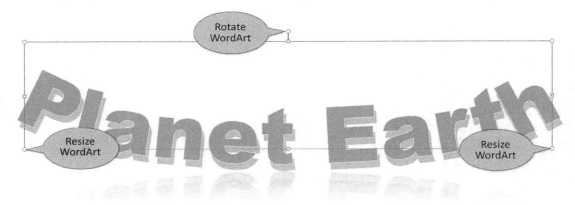

5 Mail Merge

In this section we'll take a look at creating a mail merge to create addressed envelopes and invites using Publisher.

For this section you'll need the files from

www.elluminetpress.com/ms-pub

Scroll down to the publisher section and download the files.

Mail Merge Envelopes

If you have a lot of recipients, creating an envelope for each of them can be time consuming. This is where mail merge comes in handy.

First, you'll need to open an envelope template or create one. On the start up screen click 'new'. Scroll down and select 'built in', then click 'envelopes'.

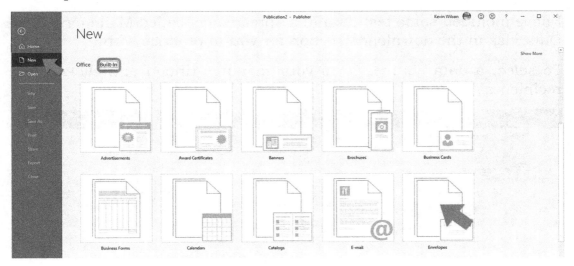

Scroll down to 'blank sizes' and select the size of envelope you're going to use. Click 'create'.

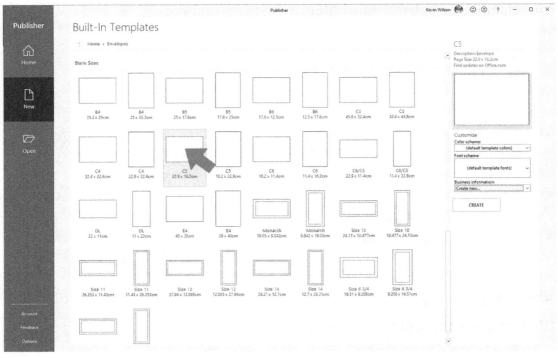

Chapter 5: Mail Merge

Next you'll need a data source. This is usually a list of names and addresses. A good place to keep names and addresses is in an excel spreadsheet. Also if you have added addresses to your Outlook 2019 contact list, you can import them from that.

I have a client list stored in an excel spreadsheet, so in this example, I will use that option. The procedure is the same if you use your Outlook contacts.

I have included some test data in a spreadsheet called Mail Merge Test Data.xlsx in the downloads section for you to practice with.

To select a data source, go to your mailings ribbon and click 'select recipients'.

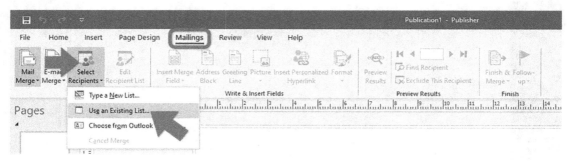

From the drop down menu, click 'use an existing list...'.

In the dialog box that appears, find your data source. I'm going to select my excel spreadsheet. Mail Merge Test Data.xlsx

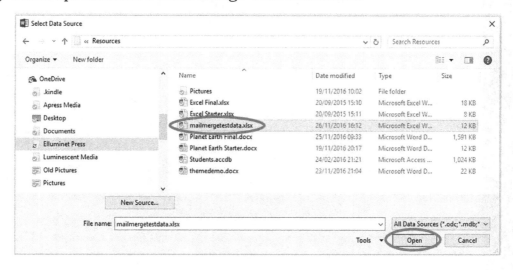

Click 'open'.

Click 'ok' on the next two dialog boxes.

Now to create your envelopes. From your mailings ribbon, click 'address block' to add the addresses from your contacts data source (Mail Merge Test Data.xlsx).

Resize your address block...

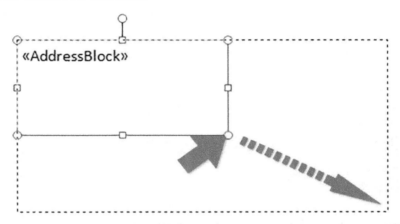

To preview your envelopes, from the mailings ribbon click 'preview results'. You can flip through the envelopes using the next/previous record icons.

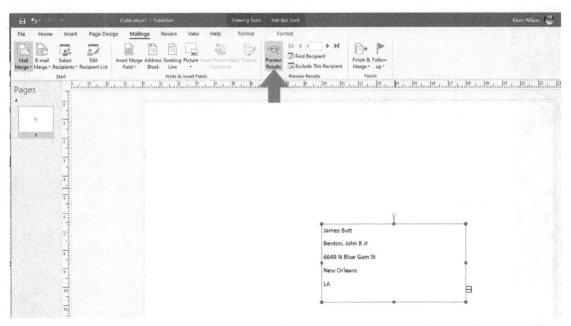

To finish off, from your mailings ribbon click 'finish & merge'. From the drop down menu, click 'print documents' to send the whole lot to the printer, make sure you have your envelopes already loaded into your printer's paper tray.

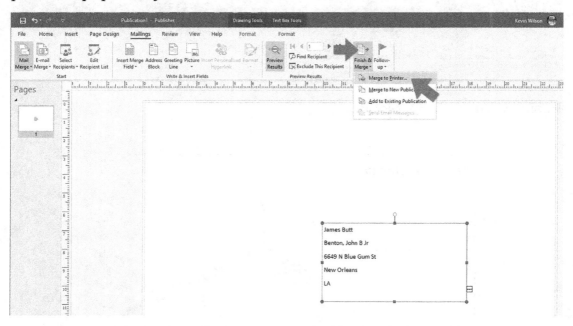

You can also click 'edit individual documents' and Word will generate a document with all your envelopes ready to print. This is useful if you want to make some changes or only print certain addresses.

Select 'print all records' from the popup dialog box.

Mail Merge an Invitation

Now that we have our envelopes printed, we need to create our party invitation.

First open a template. On publisher's start screen, click 'new'. In the search field type in the publication template you want, in this example I'm creating a party invitation, so I'd type in 'party invitation'.

Double click the template you want.

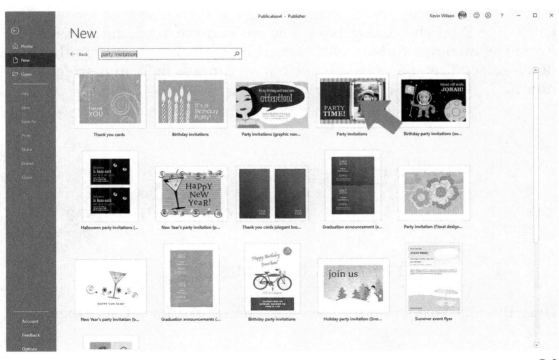

Next you need to add your data source. To connect your data source, select your mailings ribbon and click 'select recipients'. From the drop down menu, select 'use an existing list'.

Then select your data file. For this example, I'm using Mail Merge Test Data.xlsx.

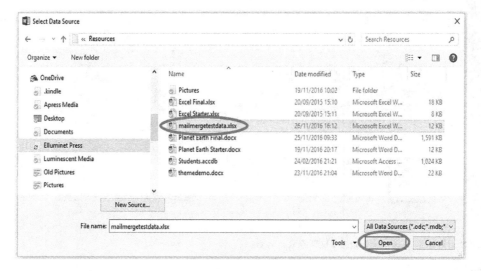

Click 'open' on the dialog box. Now we can start adding our names. From the mailings ribbon, click 'insert merge field', then from the drop down select 'first_name', then click 'insert merge field' and select 'last_name'.

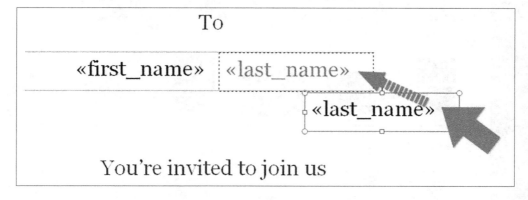

Drag the text boxes into position and change the font if necessary.

Once you have added all the fields, from the mailings ribbon click 'preview results'. You'll get something like this (a personalised invitation for each name):

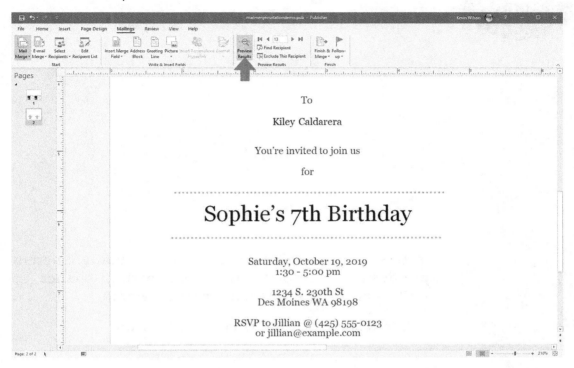

To finish off, from the mailings ribbon, click 'finish & merge'

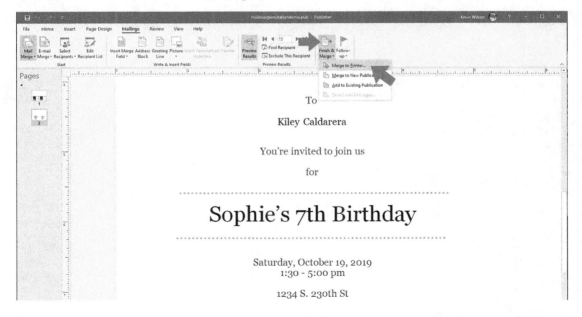

To send all letters to the printer click, 'print documents'.

Using Templates

In this section, we'll take a look at the many different pre-designed templates that come with publisher, as well as creating a template from scratch.

For this section you'll need the files from

www.elluminetpress.com/ms-pub

Scroll down to the publisher section and download the files.

Finding a Template

When you start Publisher, you will see a screen containing thumbnails of different templates that are available. To find templates, click 'new' on the left hand side.

The best way to find templates is to search for them.

Why not try making a greeting card for someone you know?

Open Publisher, click 'new' on the left hand side and type...

`greeting card`

...into the search field.

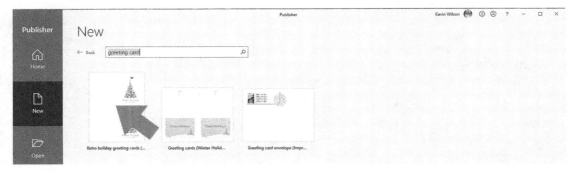

Select a template to use from the search results. How about a nice Christmas card?

Double click the template thumbnail.

Chapter 6: Using Templates

You can change the text or photo

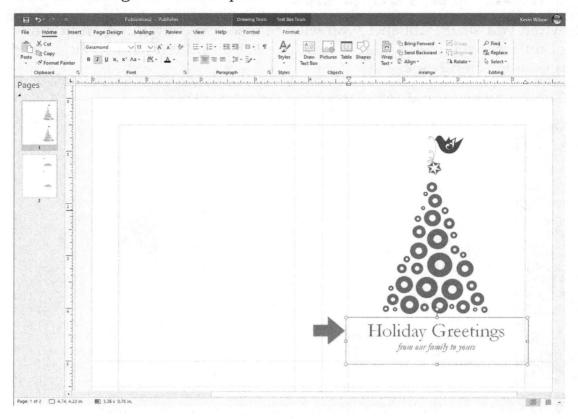

Just click on the text and enter your own.

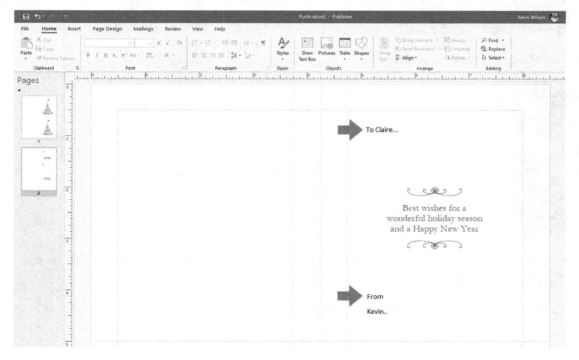

Making Your Own Template

If you have created your own style, eg heading sizes, fonts and layouts, you can save this as a template, so you can create new documents in the same style.

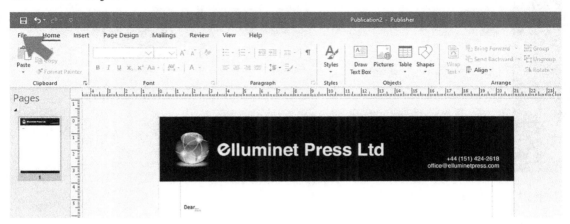

To save your publication as a template, select 'file' on the top left. From the backstage menu, select 'save as'. Select your 'onedrive' folder.

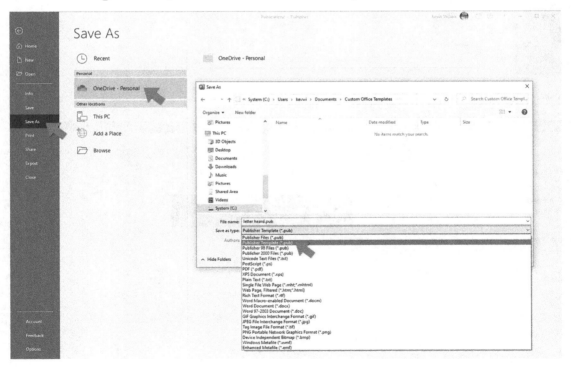

From the popup 'save as' dialog box, go down to 'save as type'. Change this to 'publisher template'

Click 'save'.

To open a new file using the template, from the publisher start screen, click 'new'.

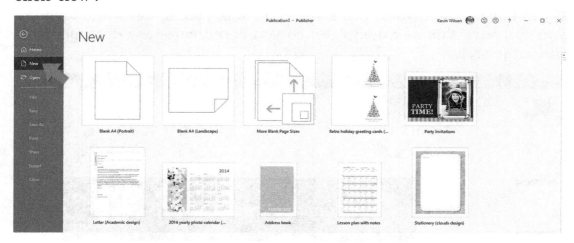

Scroll down and select 'personal'.

Double click your template. Now you can type in your text.

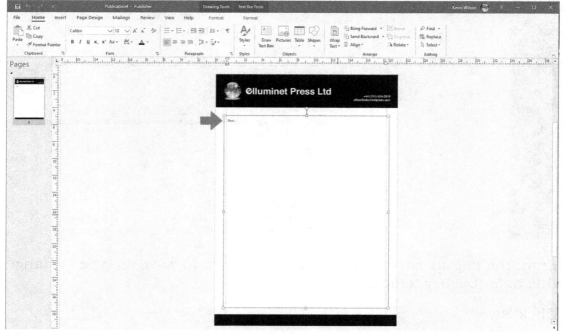

Save as a new publication. To do this, click 'file' on the top left of the screen.

Click 'save as'.

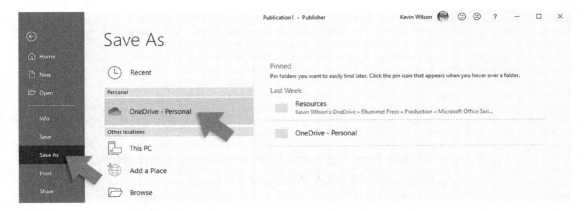

Select a folder to save your document in, and give the file a meaningful name.

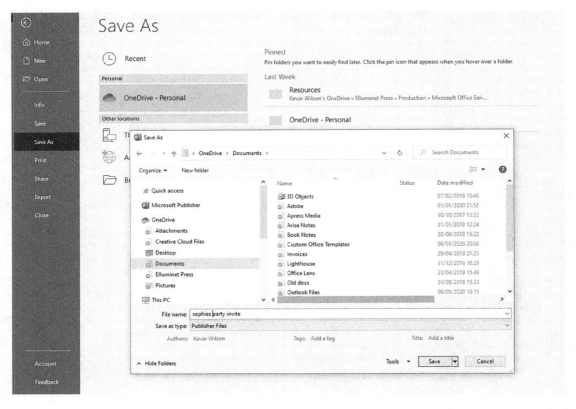

Managing Publications

In this section we'll look at saving your work, printing, page setup and page masters.

For this section you'll need the files from

www.elluminetpress.com/ms-pub

Scroll down to the publisher section and download the files.

Saving Documents

To save your work, click the small disk icon in the top left hand corner of the screen.

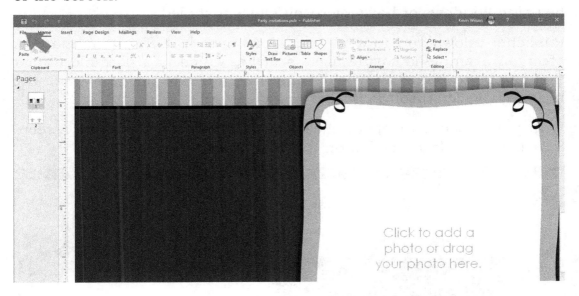

Click 'save as' on the left hand side. In the save as screen, you need to tell Publisher where you want to save the document. Double click on your OneDrive then from the dialog box, select where you want to save your publication (eg in 'documents').

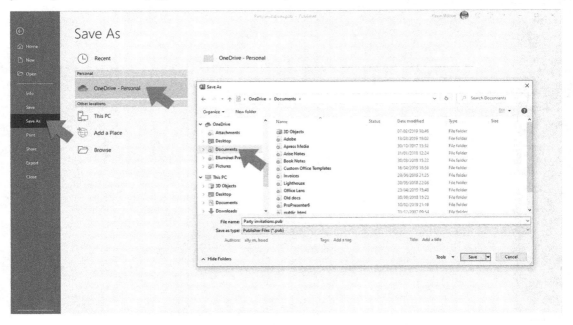

Give your file a name, in this case 'party invitations'. Click 'save'.

Saving as a Different Format

Sometimes you'll want to save a document in a different format. This can be useful if you are sending a document to someone that might not be using Windows or have Microsoft Office installed.

Publisher allows you to save your document in different formats. A common example is saving files as PDFs, which is a portable format that can be read on any type of computer, tablet or phone without the need to have Microsoft Publisher installed.

With your document open, click File on the top left of your screen. Select 'save as' from the list on the left hand side.

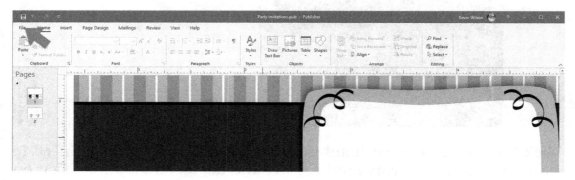

Double click 'OneDrive', select the folder you want to save the document into. Eg 'documents'.

Give your file a name, in this case 'party invitations'.

Now to change the format, click the down arrow in the field below and from the list, click PDF.

Select 'options' on the bottom left of the dialog box.

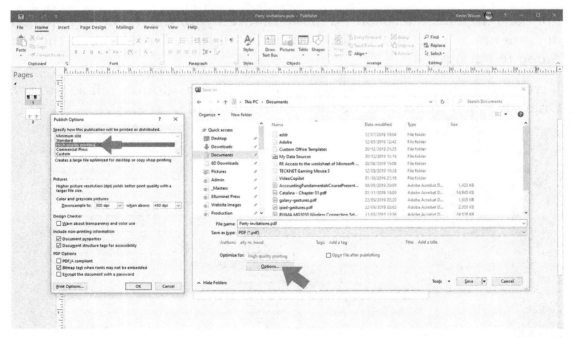

Select high quality printing, then click 'ok'. Click 'save' on the 'save as' dialog box.

Opening Saved Documents

If Publisher is already open you can open previously saved documents by clicking the 'file' menu on the top left of your screen.

From the green bar along the left hand side click 'open'.

From the list, select the document you want to open. The document from the previous project was saved as 'party invitations.pub', so this is the one I am going to open here.

For convenience, Microsoft Publisher lists all your most recently opened documents. Your latest files will be listed first. Double click the file name to open it.

If your document is saved on your OneDrive, double click on the OneDrive icon to browse the files. Select your file.

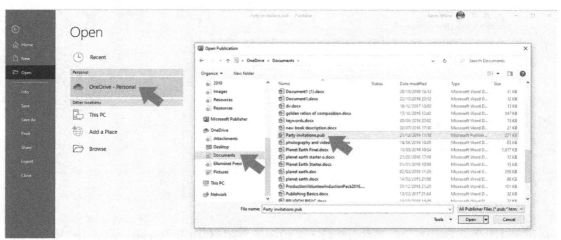

Click 'open'.

104

Page Setup

Page setup allows you to adjust margins, paper size, orientation (landscape/portrait) and general layout.

To adjust your page setup, go to your 'page design' tab and click the expand icon on the bottom right of the page setup section.

From the dialog box that appears, you can adjust the layout type meaning you can create a booklet layout, envelope, full page, etc

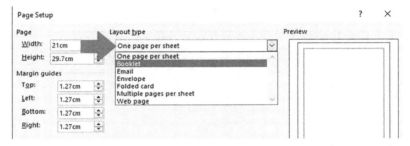

You can adjust the margins as shown below using the 'margin guides'.

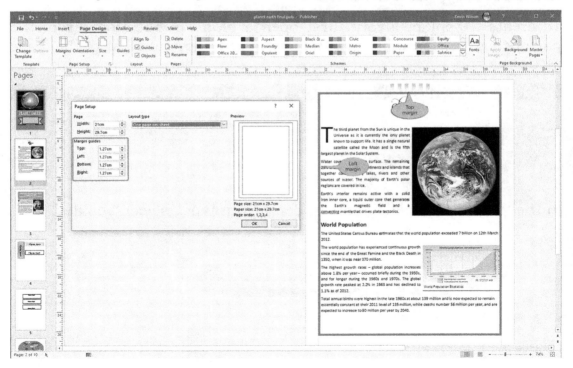

You can also adjust the page size.

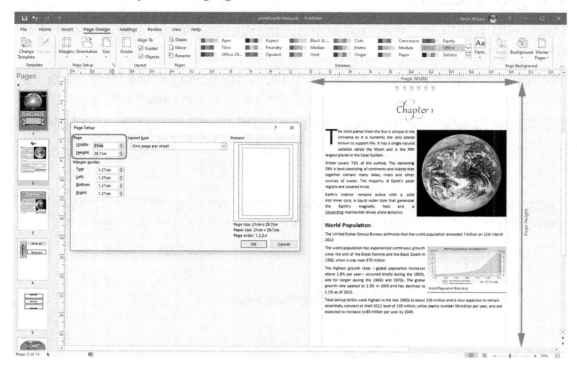

Creating Booklets

To create a booklet layout, first open a blank publication. From the page design ribbon tab, click the icon on the bottom right of the 'page setup' section.

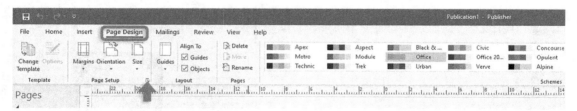

In the 'page setup' dialog box, under 'layout type', select 'booklet'.

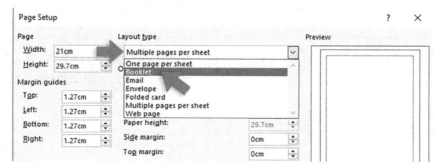

Once you click 'ok', Publisher will create a booklet layout for you. On the left hand side of your screen you'll see your pages in the navigation pane. Here, you have your front page, then the inside spread and the back page.

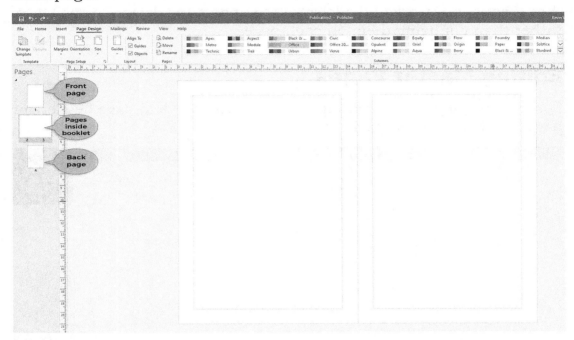

Now you can start to build your booklet. This is the best way to start. If you convert a publisher document to booklet form you may have problems with layout if publisher needs to resize pages.

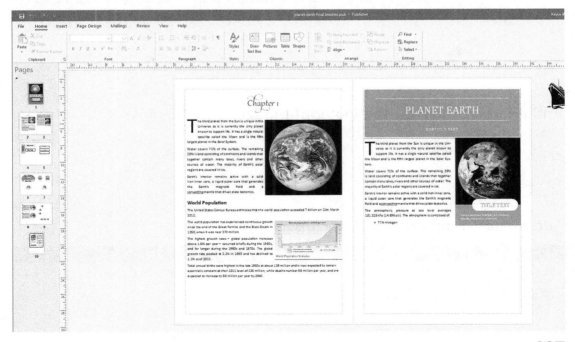

Page Masters

Page Masters allow you to repeat design and layout elements on multiple pages in a publication. This creates a more consistent appearance throughout your work and allows you to update the design in one place, rather than changing them on each page.

Editing Master Pages

For example, if you are creating a booklet, you can add page headers or page numbers to each page.

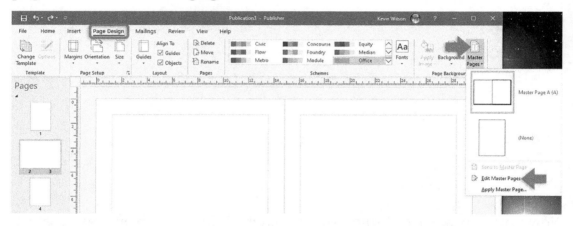

Add a header such as a title.

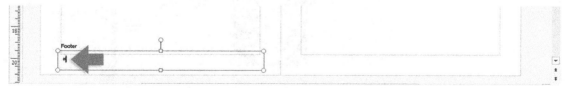

Add a footer. Click on the footer of the page.

Add a page number, click 'insert page number'.

Creating Master Pages

To create a new master, select the 'page design' ribbon tab, then click 'add master page'.

Give the master a descriptive name in the 'description' field. Click 'ok'.

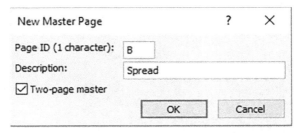

If you want the master to be a two page spread, one you'd find in the middle of a booklet, click 'two-page master'. If you just want an individual page, un-tick this option.

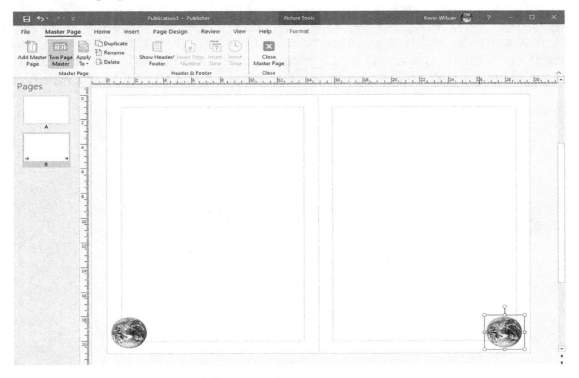

Now, build your master. You can insert pictures or text boxes as normal using the 'insert' ribbon tab.

Applying Masters

To apply a master to a page, right click on the page or spread in the page navigation pane on the left hand side. Go down to 'master pages' and select a master from the slideout menu.

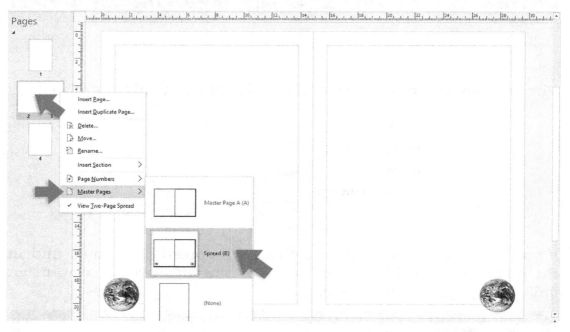

If you want to apply a master to a range of pages or multiple pages, right click on the page in the page navigation pane on the left. Go down to 'master pages', select 'apply master pages' from the slideout menu.

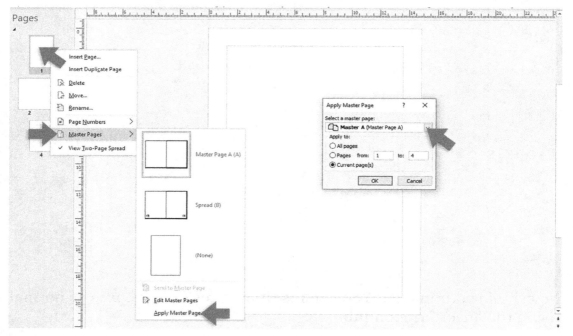

From the dialog box, select the master you want to apply

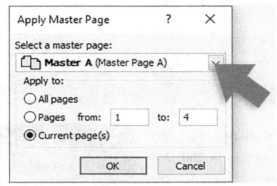

Select which pages want to apply the master to, eg 'all pages'. Click 'ok'.

Guides

Layout guides help you space out your publication, align pictures, text boxes, and tables. Layout guides appear on your page as a line or grid.

There are pre-set guides you can use to layout your publication. To enable them, select your 'page design' ribbon tab and click 'guides'.

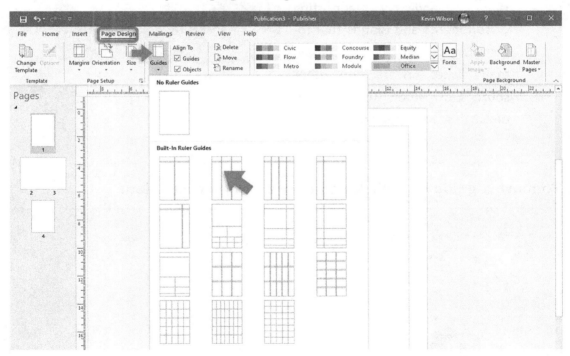

From the drop down menu you can select the layout you want. For example, if you're creating a newsletter select a two or three column guide.

Align your text boxes, headings and pictures to the grid lines.

PLANET EARTH

The third planet from the Sun is unique in the Universe as it is currently the only planet known to support life. It has a single natural satellite called the Moon and is the fifth largest planet in the Solar System.

Water covers 71% of the surface. The remaining 29% is land consisting of continents and islands that together contain many lakes, rivers and other sources of water. The majority of Earth's polar regions are cov-

EARTH

This is a good place to briefly, but effectively, describe your product or

To move a guide line, click and drag it to a new position.

To add a guide line, click on the vertical ruler and drag the green guide line into position on the page.

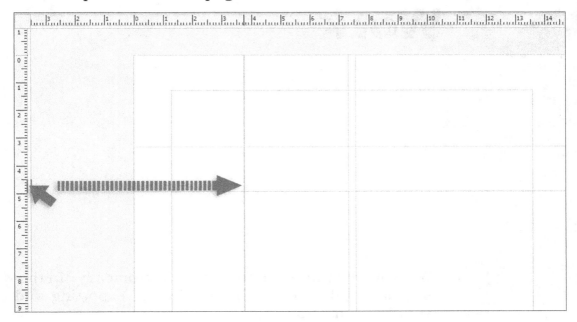

For horizontal guides, click the horizontal ruler and drag the green guide down into position on the page.

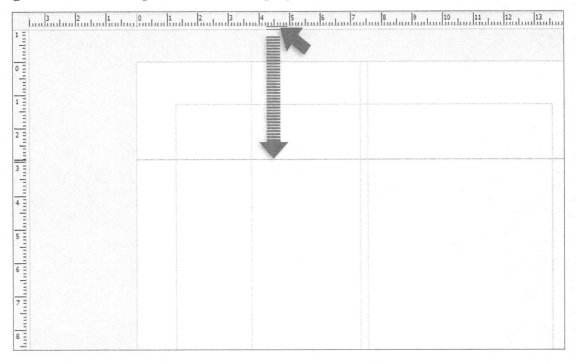

To delete a guide line, right click on the line and select 'delete guide'

Publishing your Work

Will you be printing? Publishing electronically? In this section, we'll take a look at printing, exporting and sharing your publications.

Printing Documents

To print a document, click 'file' on the top left of your screen.

Select 'print' from the green bar along the left of the screen.

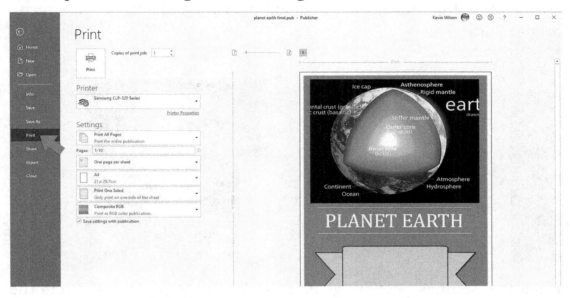

You can select options such as number of copies, print individual pages or print all pages.

You can print the page on one sheet of paper or scale it up to multiple sheets. Or you can print multiple pages on a single sheet. You can also print the pages into a booklet. To change this setting click the 'one page per sheet' drop down menu.

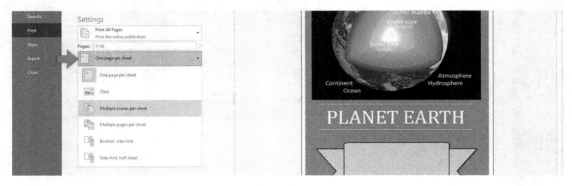

Once you have set all your options, click the print button at the top.

Print as Booklet

Open your publication. To print as a booklet, select 'file' on the top left of the screen,

Select 'print' from the green bar along the left hand side of the screen.

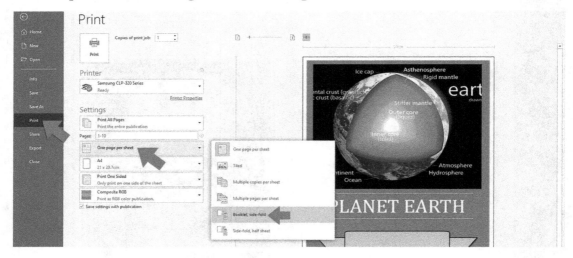

From the 'settings' section, go down to 'one page per sheet'. From the popup menu, select 'booklet side fold'.

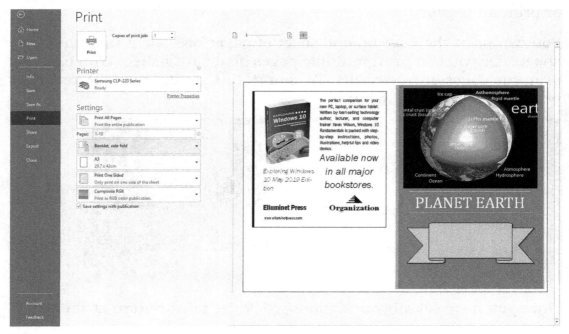

Most modern printers support duplex printing (ie printing on both sides of the paper). With some desktop printers, choosing duplex means that the printer prints all of the copies of the first side of a page, then pauses and asks you to flip the sheets that it just printed and return them to the printer. Then it prints all of the copies of the second side.

To print on both sides, click the drop down box that says 'print one sided'

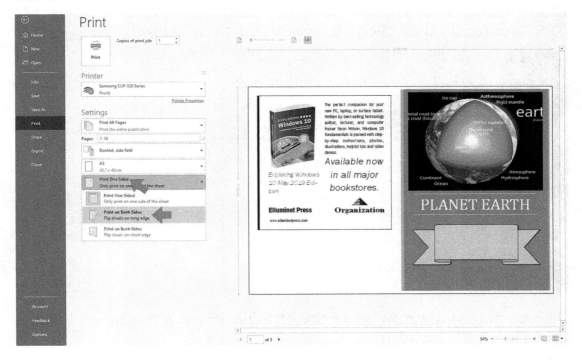

Click 'print' at the top of the screen.

If printing on both sides of the page, once the printer has printed the first side, turn the whole stack of printed sheets over and put them back into the paper tray.

Export as PDF

Click File on the top left of your screen.

Select 'export' from the list on the left hand side. Select 'create PDF/XPS Document', then click the 'create PDF/XPS' button.

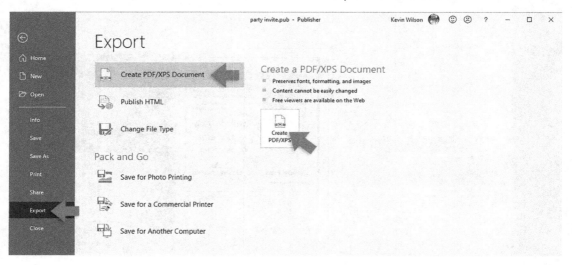

Select where you want to save the PDF file, give it a meaningful name, then click 'publish'.

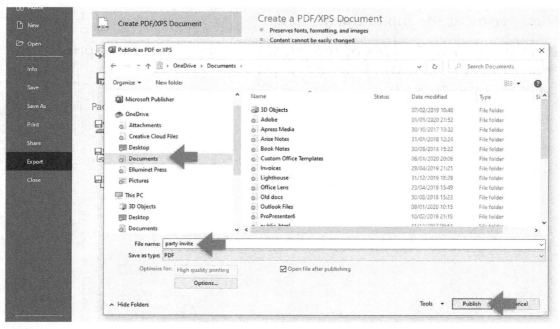

Share a File

Click File on the top left of your screen.

Select 'share' from the list on the left hand side.

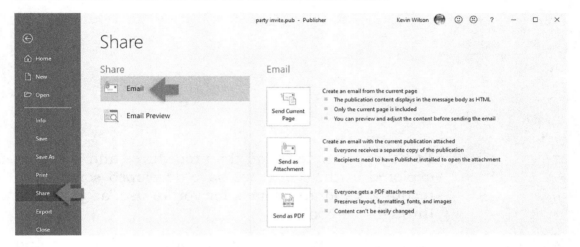

Now select how you want to attach the file to your email. You can send the current page as an email, you can send your publication as a publisher file (.pub), or you can send the file as a PDF. If you are sending the file to someone who doesn't have publisher installed, you should send the file as a PDF.

In this example I'm going to send as PDF. So I'd click 'send as PDF'. Once the email opens up, you'll see the file attached to the email. Add the email address of the person you're sending the file to, add a subject and a message.

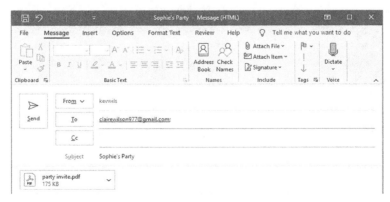

Click 'send' when you're done.

Resources

To help you understand the procedures and concepts explored in this book, we have developed some video resources and app demos for you to use, as you work through the book.

To find the resources, open your web browser and navigate to the following website

www.elluminetpress.com/ms-pub

At the beginning of each chapter, you'll find a website that contains the resources for that chapter.

File Resources

To save the files into your OneDrive documents folder, right click on the icons above and select 'save target as' (or 'save link as', on some browsers). In the dialog box that appears, select 'OneDrive', click the 'Documents' folder, then click 'save'.

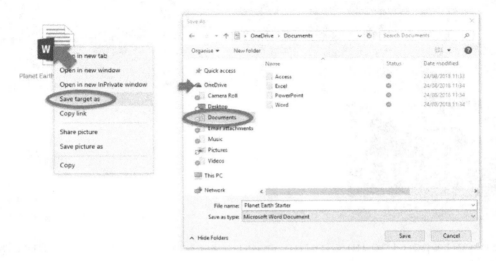

The sample images are stored in a compressed zip file. To download the zip file, right click on the zip icon on the page above, 'Sample Images. zip. Select 'save target as' (or 'save link as', on some browsers) and save it into 'pictures' on your OneDrive folder.

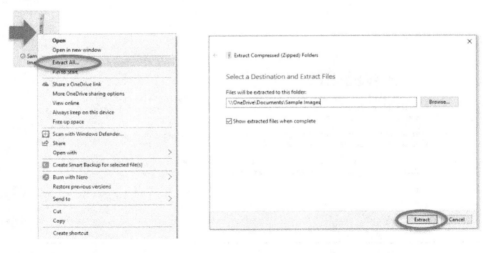

Once you have downloaded the zip file, go to your 'pictures' folder in your OneDrive, right click on the zip file, and select 'extract all' from the menu. From the dialog box that appears click 'extract'. This will create a new folder in your pictures called 'sample images'. You'll find the images used in the examples in the books.

Video Resources

The video resources are grouped into sections for each chapter in the book. Click the thumbnail link to open the section.

Getting Started

Building Documents

Managing Documents

Images, Tables & Charts

Document Templates

When you open the link to the video resources, you'll see a thumbnail list at the bottom.

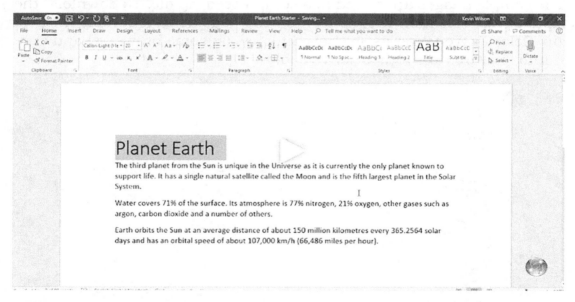

Click on the thumbnail for the particular video you want to watch. Most videos are between 30 and 60 seconds outlining the procedure, others are a bit longer.

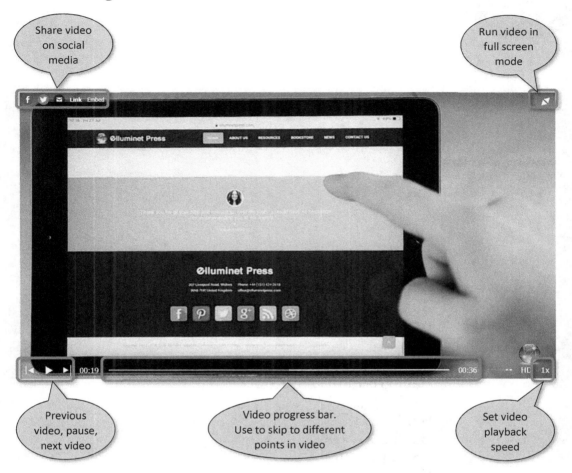

When the video is playing, hover your mouse over the video and you'll see some controls...

Index

Index